# V. J. M.ʸ J.

Viva Jesus, María y José

# V.J.

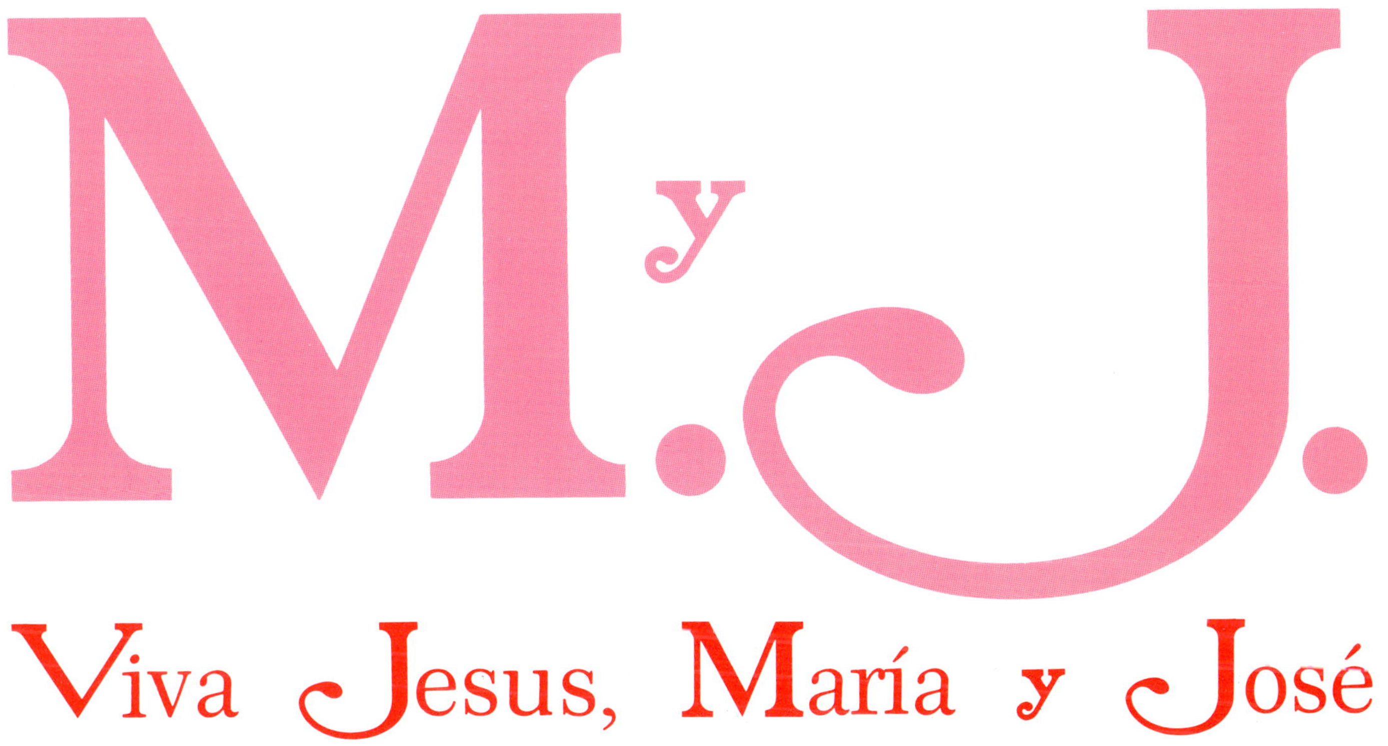


# Viva Jesus, María y José

## A Celebration of the Birth of Jesus

Mexican Folk Art and Toys from the Collection of Robert K. Winn

Foreword by Everett H. Jones

Photographs by Michael J. Smith

Trinity University Press • San Antonio, Texas

*The Trinity University Press gratefully acknowledges the assistance of Mr. and Mrs. Marshall Terrell Steves in making this book possible.*


Library of Congress Catalog Card Number 77-089457
SBN # 911536-68-X
Printed in the United States of America
Printed by Best Printing Company
Bound by Custom Bookbinders
Typesetting by G & S Typesetters, Inc.

Photography by Michael J. Smith

# *Acknowledgments*

To list the names of all who contributed to this book is impossible, but the following persons deserve special recognition.

Humberto Arellano Garza of Monterrey was an excellent teacher and guide in my collecting of Mexican folk art after World War II. Alexander Girard mounted a superb exhibit in 1962 of his collection of international nativities in Kansas City, which was my inspiration to concentrate on Mexican folk art celebrating the birth of Jesus. My work with Mr. Girard on the installation of "The Magic of the People" for Hemisfair '68 in San Antonio, Texas, was an incentive to further study. Kathleen Gallander, director of the Art Museum of South Texas in Corpus Christi, is responsible for my original organization and presentation of an exhibit of *V. J. M. y J.* in the Art Museum of South Texas in December, 1972.

Patsy Steves has been a source of continuing inspiration and interest in my presentation of the collection. Her love of Mexican folk art and her knowledgeability in developing her own collection has provided a beneficial association for me. Marshall Steves made the publication of this book possible as a gift to Patsy, his wife, for Christmas 1976.

My mother and father, Ethel and Murray Winn, are the greatest contributors, for they showed me beautiful things in Mexico when I was in my pre-teens.

Finally, the artists who created the works are mostly unknown, but each of them is surely a contributor. My hope is that a sincere understanding of the spirit of Christmas and a love for the folk art of Mexico will be felt by all who peruse these pages.

Robert K. Winn
San Antonio, Texas

# *Foreword*

All through Christian history there has been a close relationship between religious worship and religious art.

The art forms have varied in different part of the world and in different periods of history. They have ranged from the elaborate paintings of the Italian Renaissance and the Gothic cathedrals of the Middle Ages to simple displays of folk art rising spontaneously out of the simple faith of simple people.

This book is the work of a writer and collector, Robert Winn, who is himself a sensitive artist. His particular interest is the religious folk art of Mexico. He has specialized in what he calls "the Mexican salutation to Christmas—a time of joy, of celebration, and of national fiestas."

Folk art has been defined in the *New Columbia Encyclopedia*, 1975 edition, as "the art works of a culturally homogenous people produced by artists without formal training." The examples in this book are also products of a homogenous religious tradition, one which finds endless fascination in the story of the birth of Christ.



Even the most callous observer will be impressed with the reverence, the devotion, and the artistic imagination revealed in these creations of Mexican artists and artisans. The various figures may have a roughhewn, awkward aspect, but they nevertheless convey a spiritual message. They are eloquent expressions of the faith which gives meaning to the life of those who created them.

As Mr. Winn points out, the Christmas folk art of Mexico grew out of a practical need: There had to be a simple and appealing way to teach the Christmas story to the Indians. From the beginning, a tradition has been maintained; it has flourished from generation to generation, with interesting innovations developed in different parts of the country and by individual artists.

Here is a book to enrich Everyman's joy in the Christmas story. Moreover, it will arouse a new appreciation for the living tradition of religious art in our neighboring republic.

Everett H. Jones
Retired Bishop of the
Episcopal Diocese of West Texas

# *Contents*

# V. J. M. y J.

Viva Jesus, María y José

# *Mexican Folk Art*

V. J. M. y J., which stands for Viva Jesus, María y José, is a Mexican salutation of the Christmas season. It is a joyous statement, proclaiming "Alleluia," and, by the use of the simple and abbreviated V. J. M. y J. on banners and signs, the people express their celebration of the birth of Jesus. Christmas in Mexico is a time of joy, of celebration, and of nationwide fiestas.

A unique aspect of the Mexican Christmas season is the use of the folk art produced by native artisans in the various celebrations and festivities in the homes and in the churches. The objects presented in this book are examples of the diverse and creative expressions of these artisans of Mexico. Using the raw materials of each craftsperson's native village or region, the artisans continue making the figures indigenous to their village tradition and use the techniques and styles handed down from generation to generation.

The Christmas folk art in Mexico was developed by the church as an early means of teaching the Christmas story to the Indians. Using the objects, such as the pregnant Mary and Joseph seeking shelter, the nativity with Jesus, Mary and Joseph, the wise men, and the shepherds, the church leaders told the story of the birth of Christ in a simple and expressive manner.

Thus, the Christmas folk art is unusual in that its primary goal is not necessarily to be decorative, although indeed it is, but it is made to be used to tell a story, to remind people of the events of the season. The objects are usually brought out only during the Christmas season and are not left out all year in the homes. Furthermore, specific objects are brought out at specific times during the Christmas season. For example, the nativity may be left out all season, but the baby Jesus is not put into his crib until Christmas Eve.

To put into context which of the art objects assembled in this book are used in relation to the various parts of the Christmas celebration of Mexico, it is necessary to describe the character of the season and relate the different types of art to those particular celebrations. In the body of the book, the illustrations are grouped according to the following periods.

*December 12, La Fiesta de la Santísima Virgen de Guadalupe.* Though lasting only one day and ushering in the Christmas season, this day commemorates the miracle in 1531 of the appearance of the brown Virgin of Guadalupe, Patroness of the Republic of Mexico. Figures of the virgin are honored in homes and churches on this day.

*December 16–24, Las Posadas.* The people make pilgrimages to Mexican homes and churches on the nights preceding the birth of Jesus. The word *posada* means the shelter, or derivatively, the inn, and *Las Posadas* symbolizes the search of Mary and Joseph for hospitality before the birth of the child. The breaking of a piñata is the climax of each evening. The piñata is made of a large clay jar decorated with colored paper. Suspended from the ceiling, the piñata finally is broken by a blindfolded child, and candy and gifts shower down. Representations of Joseph and the pregnant Mary are carried in the *Posada,* but the figure of the baby Jesus is never used at this time.

*December 24, La Noche Buena, The Good Night.* At midnight, *La Misa del*

*Gallo,* the Mass of the Cock, heralding the birth of Jesus, and *La Acostada,* the laying of the child in the manger, are held. The nativities displayed for this event are made of many materials: wood, clay, straw, palm, and others, depending on the region where the piece of art is made.

*December 25, Christmas Day*. This day is generally a day of recovery from the nine nights of the *posadas* and is the beginning of the twelve days of Christmas.

*December 26, Los Pastores*. The miracle play is presented. The plot follows the shepherd's journey to Bethlehem to see the newborn Jesus. During the journey, the audience is told of the Creation, the fall of Lucifer, the fall of Adam and Eve, and the formation of the seven deadly sins. At the end of the play, the shepherds pay homage to the Christ child. Masks representing the devils, angels, and shepherds are used in the production.

*January 6, El Día de los Santos Reyes, the Day of the Kings*. For this day of gift-giving, the children have written notes to the three kings expressing their gift wishes and have left the notes in their shoes placed near windows, convenient for the kings to fill. Representations of the three kings are used during this period, although the kings also are made to be used as a part of the nativity scene.

*February 2, Candelmas, The Mass of the Candles.* The season ends with the taking up of the little Jesus and the Purification of the Virgin Mary. This day is considered to be the beginning of the flight into Egypt, and the art showing this event is fashioned in both a realistic and abstract manner, according to the provenance of the object.

The folk art in this book is primarily contemporary, that is, it has been made since the 1940's. However, the objects, contemporary or old, are similar, because they continue to be made in the same style of the generations preceding the current artisan. The folk art shows a blend of technique and representation of subject matter dating from the pre-conquest and the time of the Spaniard and Spanish culture. Added to the techniques of the pre-conquest era, for example, are the methods introduced by the Spaniard, such as turning on the potter's wheel and glazing.

That each area, each village, has a distinctive style of folk art is largely determined by both the history of art in the region and the specific raw materials indigenous to the area. Fortunately for the knowledgeable collector, because each village creates in a style independent from others, it is fairly easy to identify where a particular piece of folk art comes from in Mexico. (A map at the back of this book shows the various states and villages mentioned in the captions.) Thus, the black clay objects from Acatlán, Puebla, can be distinguished from the black clay objects from Coyotepec, Oaxaca, because each of these two regions continues the tradition of its own art. Furthermore, if the artisans move to another village, they will adapt to the creations of the village rather than to express their own individual technique.

The art usually is produced by families working together. It is rarely produced in factories or in common workshops, although in some places artisans may meet in a common spot, such as the backroom of someone's house. Generally the work is done at the homes of the artisans.

As for raw materials, the artisans use what is available and except in a few cases, they do not import from one area to another. One exception would be the Tzintzuntzan ceramics where the terra cotta clay of Tzintzuntzan is slipped with a cream-colored clay which is brought from another village.

Contemporary folk art in Mexico is still being produced in the same villages by descendants of earlier artisans. However, with the increased mobility of young people who are leaving the villages, the traditional folk art will inevitably decline, although attempts are being made to keep tradition alive.

The artisans who produce the folk art, and particularly that of the Christmas season shown in this book, have common characteristics: creative and artistic instincts, highly developed manual dexterity, a sense of the traditions of native tastes and legends, reverence, and the influence of many centuries. The art objects reflect the life of the artisans, the life of the villages, the life of the country, and these articles remain the Mexicans' unique contribution to the civilization of their country.

# V.J.M.y J.

*December 12*

La Fiesta de la Santísima Virgen de Guadalupe. The beginning of the Christmas season.

*Virgin of Guadalupe and Juan Diego,* enameled terra cotta, Tlaquepaque, State of Jalisco, Madonna 12″ high. The image of the Guadalupe is so highly respected that a realistic artistic rendering is nearly always presented. The figure of Juan Diego represents the legend that an Indian saw the first apparition of the Virgin.

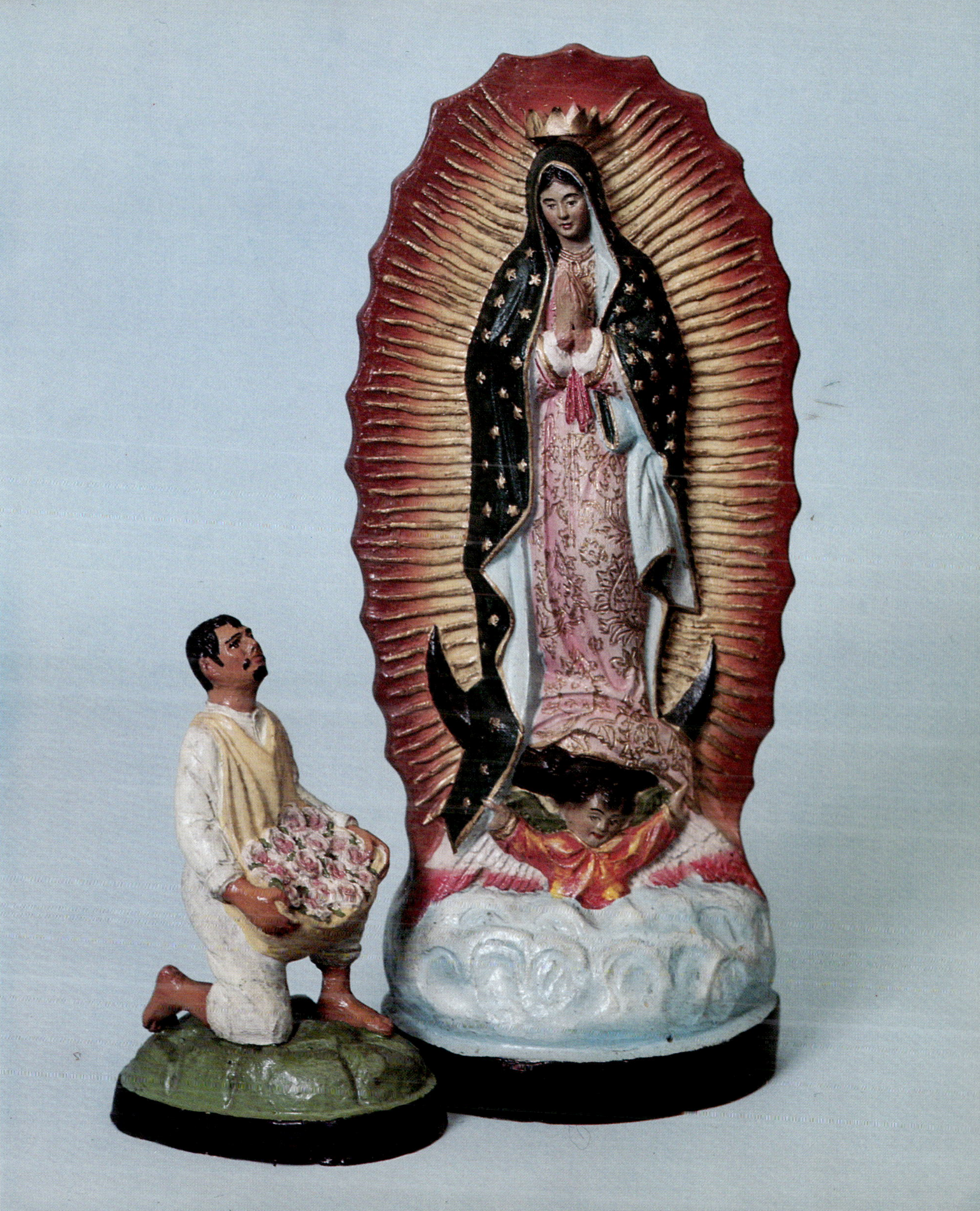

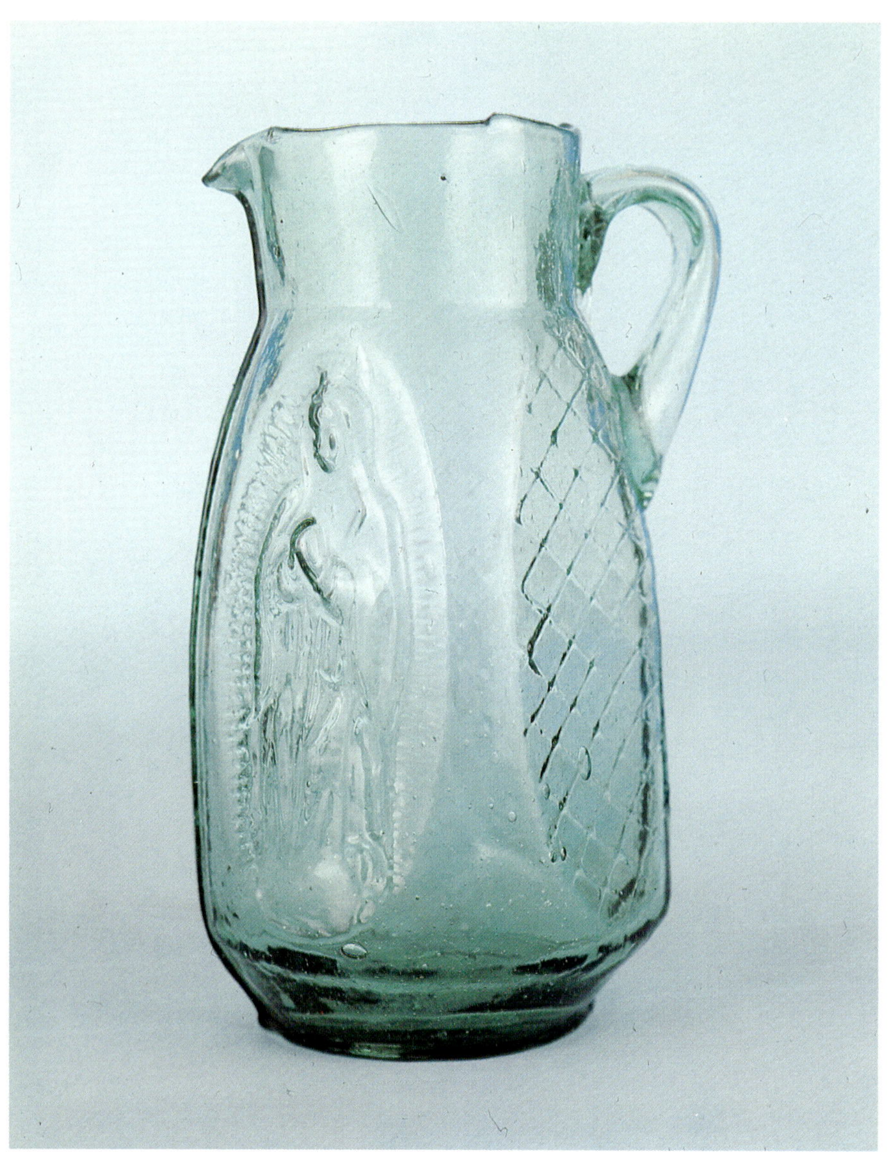

*Guadalupe Pitcher,* recycled "Coke" bottle glass, Puebla, State of Puebla, 9″ high. The image of the Guadalupe is on one side of the pitcher and Juan Diego on the other. The pitcher may be used all-year round, and the image of the Virgin on it is said to protect the liquid inside.

12

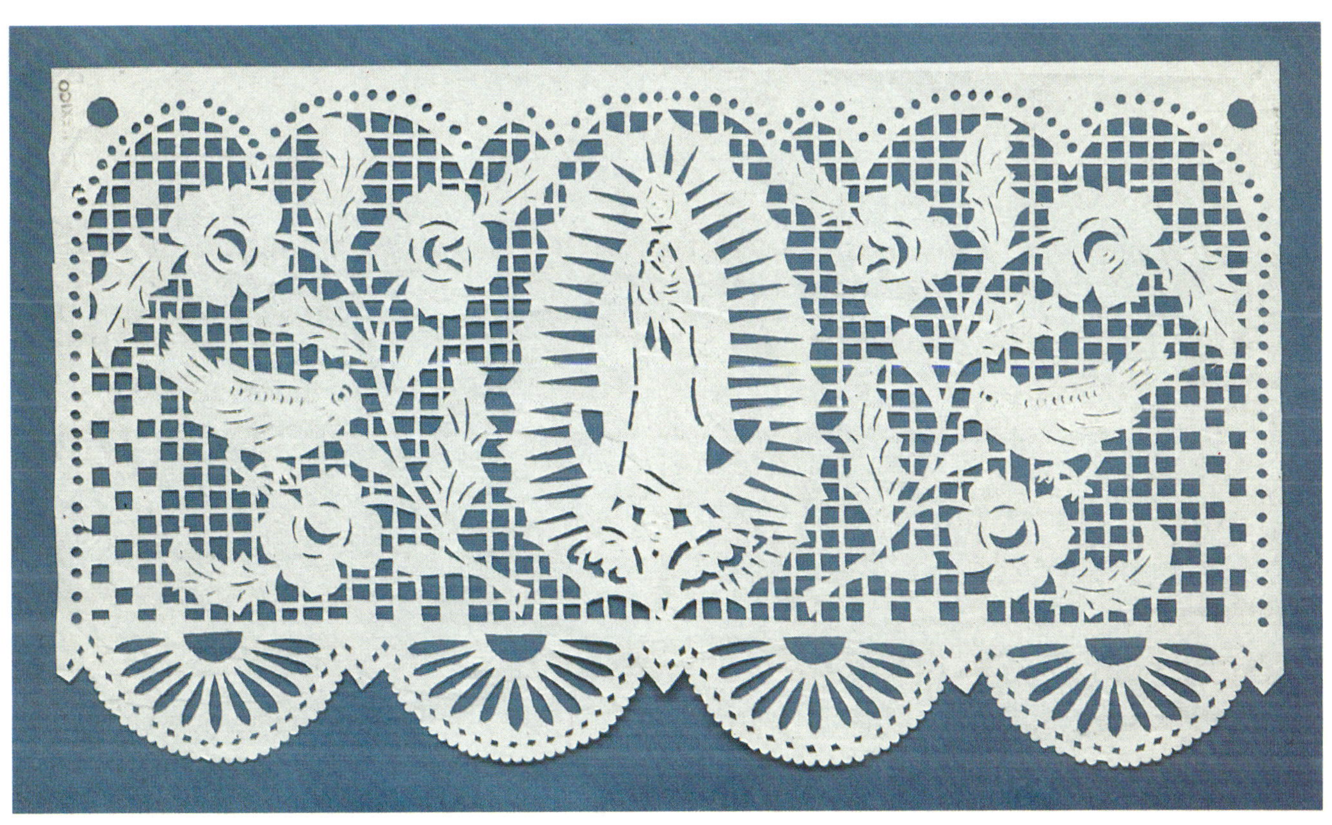

*Guadalupe Banner,* cut tissue paper, Puebla, State of Puebla, 16″ high. Banners of this type, usually in pastel colors or white, are pasted to string and hung across doorways and streets during the fiesta. The white roses on this banner represent the roses that supposedly fell from the cape of Juan Diego when he told the head of the Church in Mexico that he had seen the apparition of the Virgin.

*Nativity with Shepherds,* painted terra cotta, Tlaquepaque, State of Jalisco, and *Cathedral,* natural bamboo, Ixmiquilpan, State of Hidalgo, 40″ high. The small figures are made partially in a mold with details added by hand. The cathedral was made as a spice shelf, but it lends itself as a setting for the adoration by the shepherds.

14

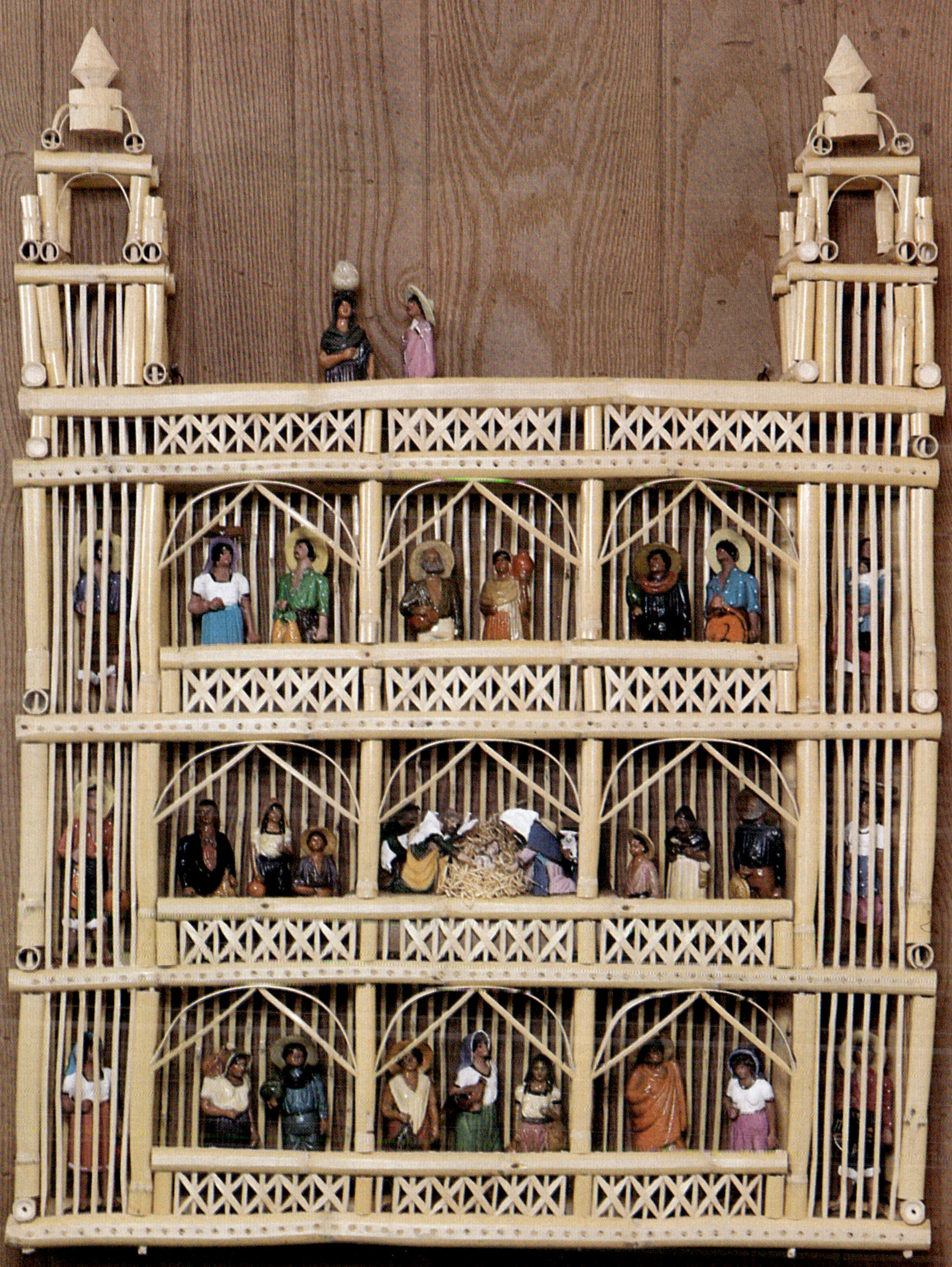

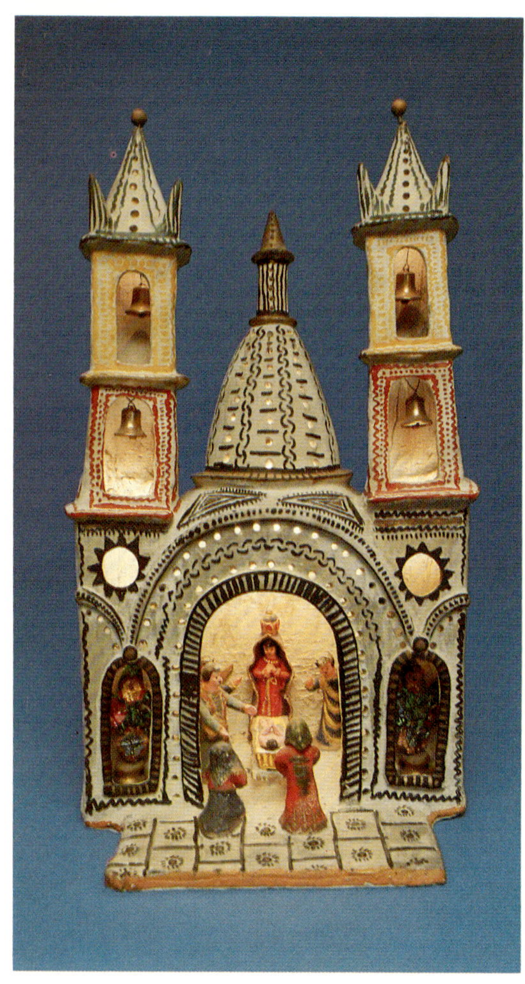

*Lighted Acatlán Church*

*Churches,* stained bamboo birdcage, 32-1/2″ high, and natural bamboo birdcage, 30″ high, Ixmiquilpan, State of Hidalgo.
*Church,* by Candelario Medrano, a well-known ceramic artist of Mexico, enameled terra cotta, Santa Cruz, State of Jalisco, 17″ high.
*Church,* stained wood, Arrasola, State of Oaxaca, 13″ high.
*Churches,* painted earthenware, Acatlán, State of Puebla, 23″ and 10″ high.

The bamboo churches are actually birdcages which are used throughout the year. During the Christmas season they are used as settings for the nativities.

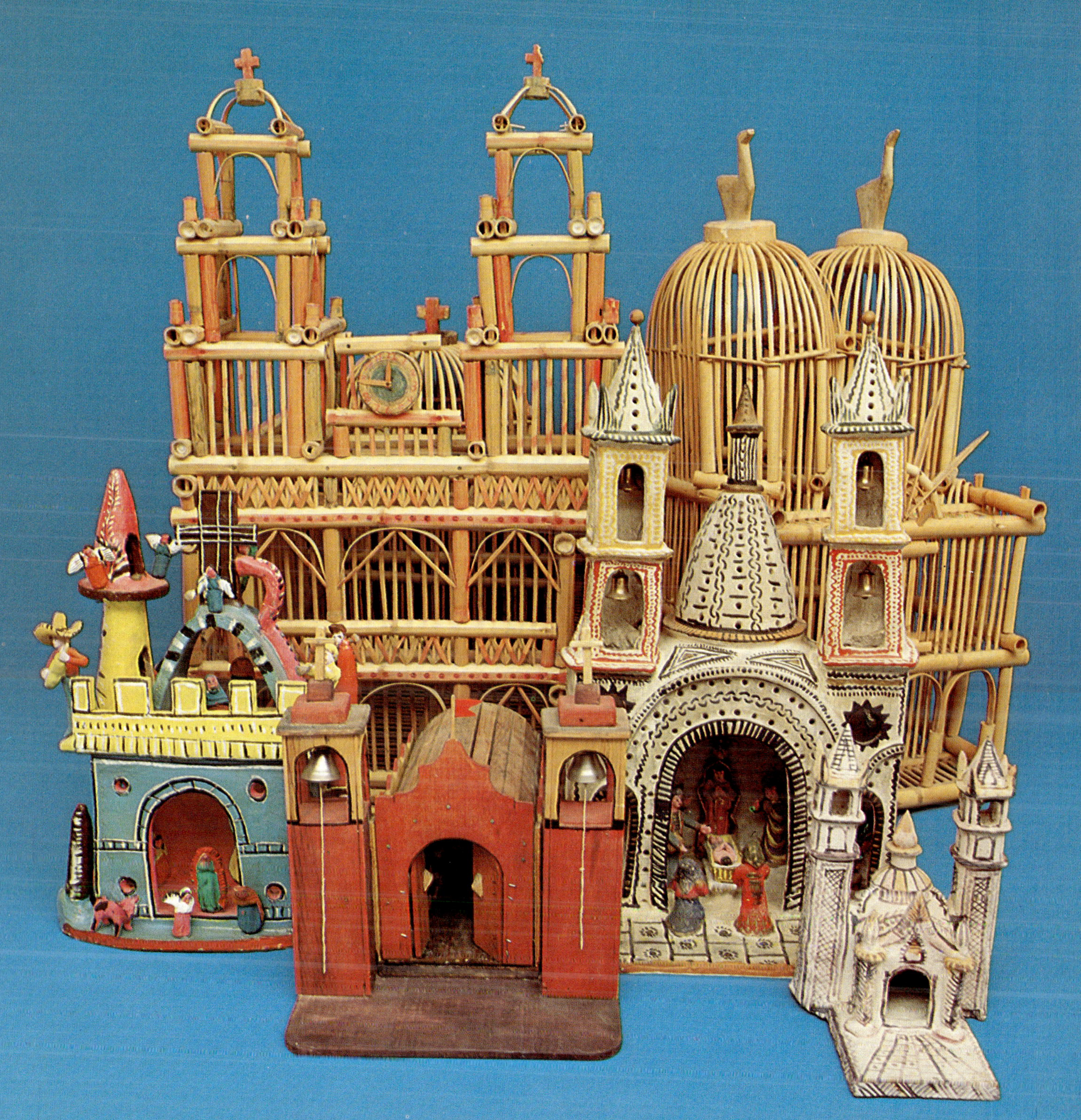

# V.J.M.<sup>y</sup>J.

*December 16–24*

Las Posadas. The search of Mary and Joseph for hospitality.

*Joseph and the pregnant Mary on their journey to Bethlehem,* painted terra cotta, Tlaquepaque, State of Jalisco, 6″ high.
*La Posada Incense Burner,* painted terra cotta, Metepec, State of México, 9-1/2″ high. Mary and Joseph await the birth of Jesus with angels in attendance.

These pieces would be on display in the home or might be carried in a *Posada* pilgrimage.

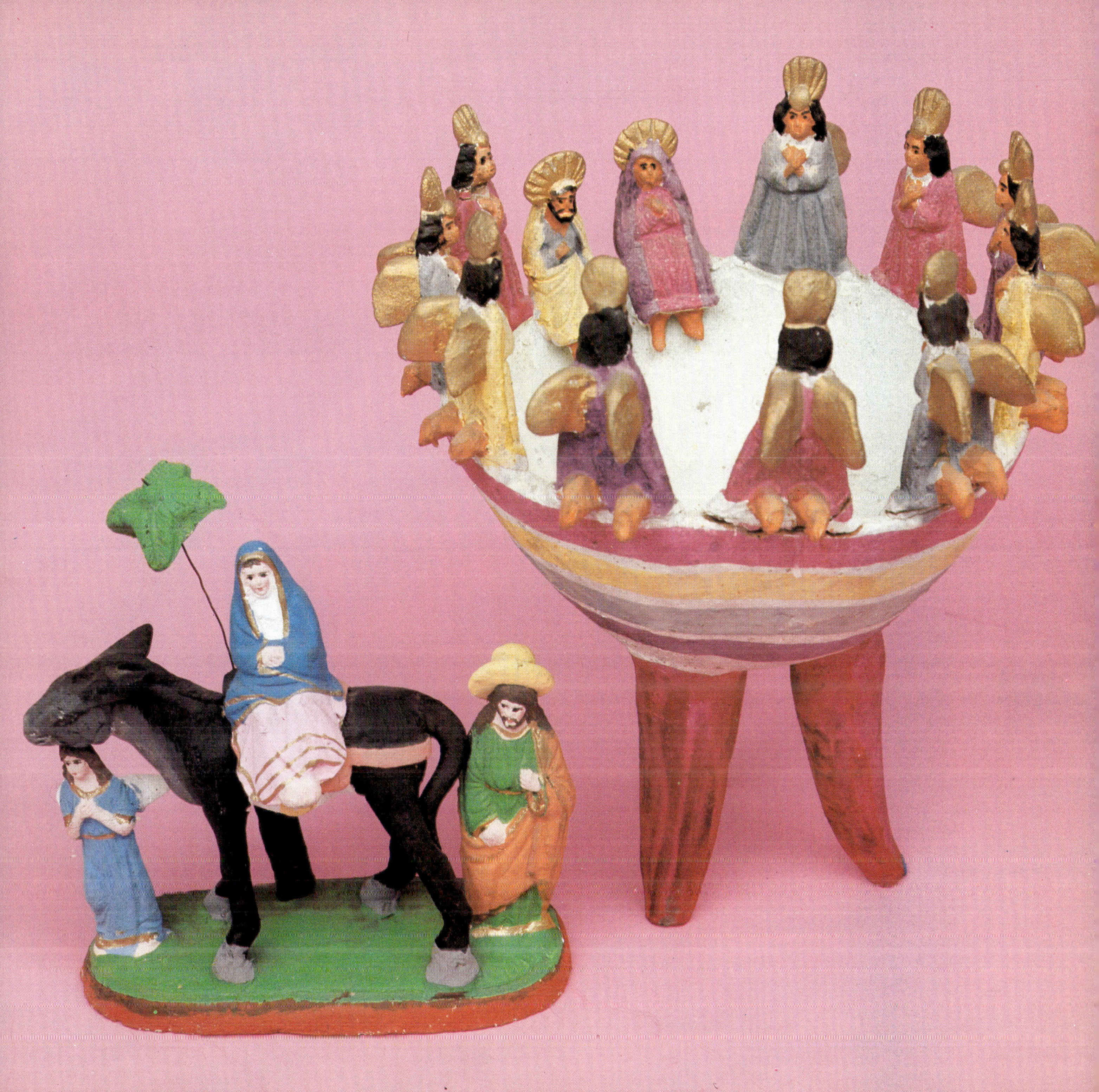

*Fantastic Nativity Arch,* painted earthenware, Acatlán, State of Puebla, 20″ high. This piece is called "fantastic" because of the many representations of the Holy Family. It is equally beautiful on both sides and could be used as a centerpiece.

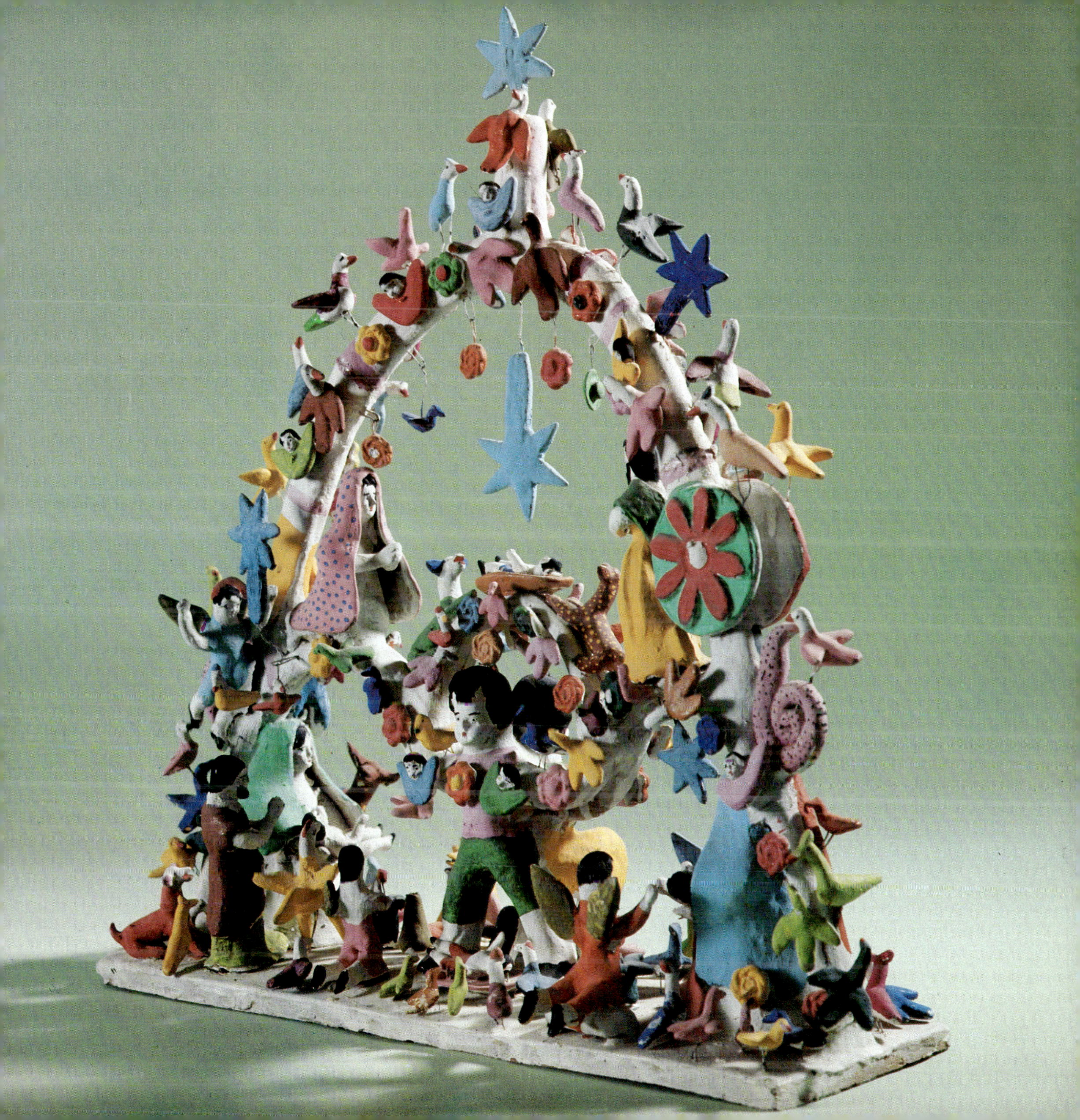

# V.J.M.y J.

*December 24*

La Noche Buena. The birth of Jesus.

*Nativity*, painted terra cotta, Metepec, State of México, Madonna 11-1/2″ high. Note the presence of El Gallo, the cock that legend said crowed at the time of the birth of Christ. On Christmas Eve, the Mass of the Cock celebrates the birth of the child, and at that time the child is actually put into the crib as a symbolic gesture.

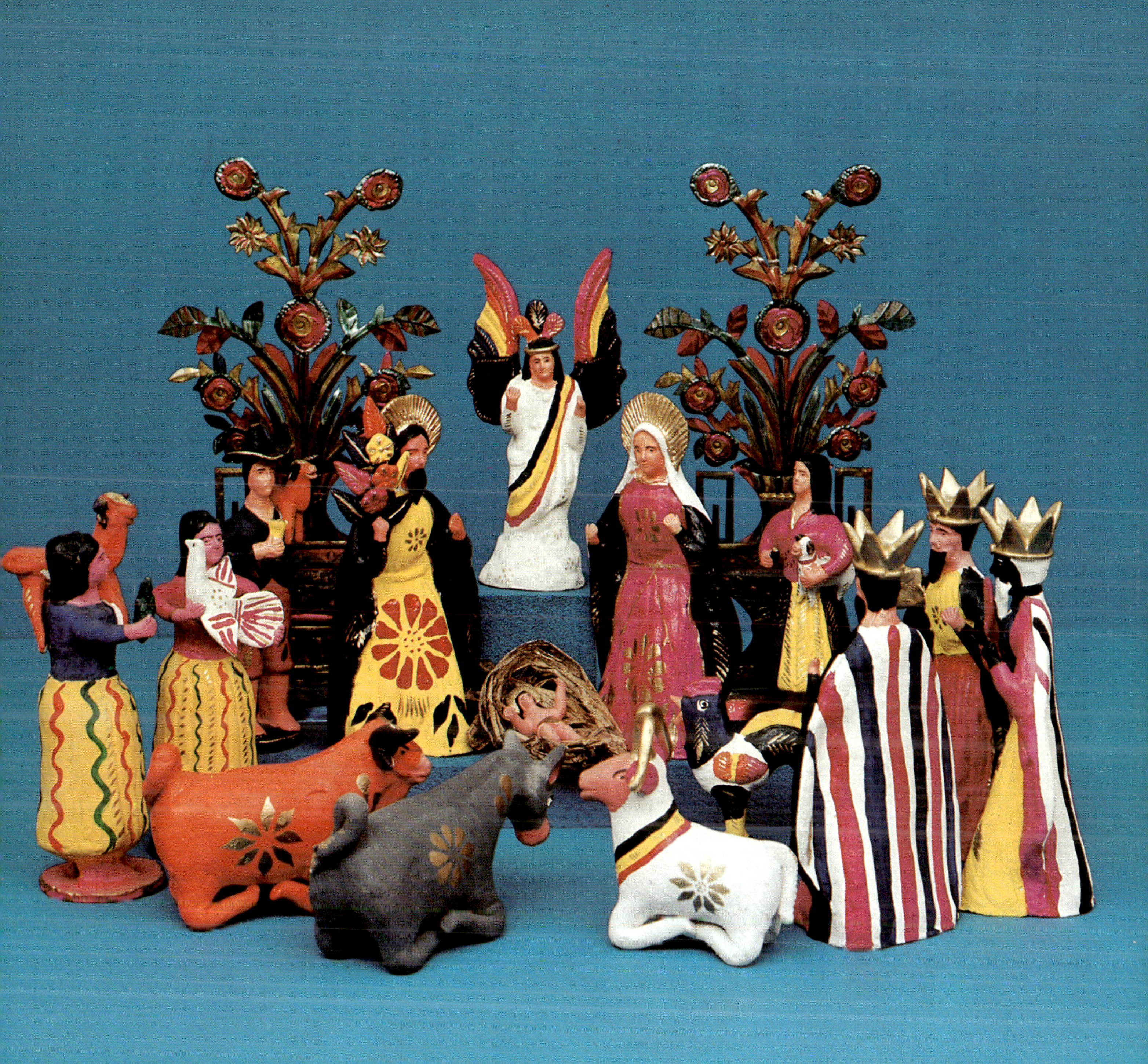

# V.J.M.y J.

*December 25*

Christmas Day. A day of recovery.

*Madonna,* by Teodora Blanco, stained earthenware, Atzompa, State of Oaxaca, 19″ high.
*Woman with lamb candelabra,* painted earthenware, Acatlán, State of Puebla, 20″ high.
*Woman with basket candle holder,* painted earthenware, Acatlán, State of Puebla, 20″ high.
*Madonna,* green glazed terra cotta, Atzompa, State of Oaxaca, 12″ high.
*Monkey with baby,* burnished black clay bottle, Coyotepec, State of Oaxaca, 12″ high.

Each town and village has its own interpretation of the Virgin Mary.

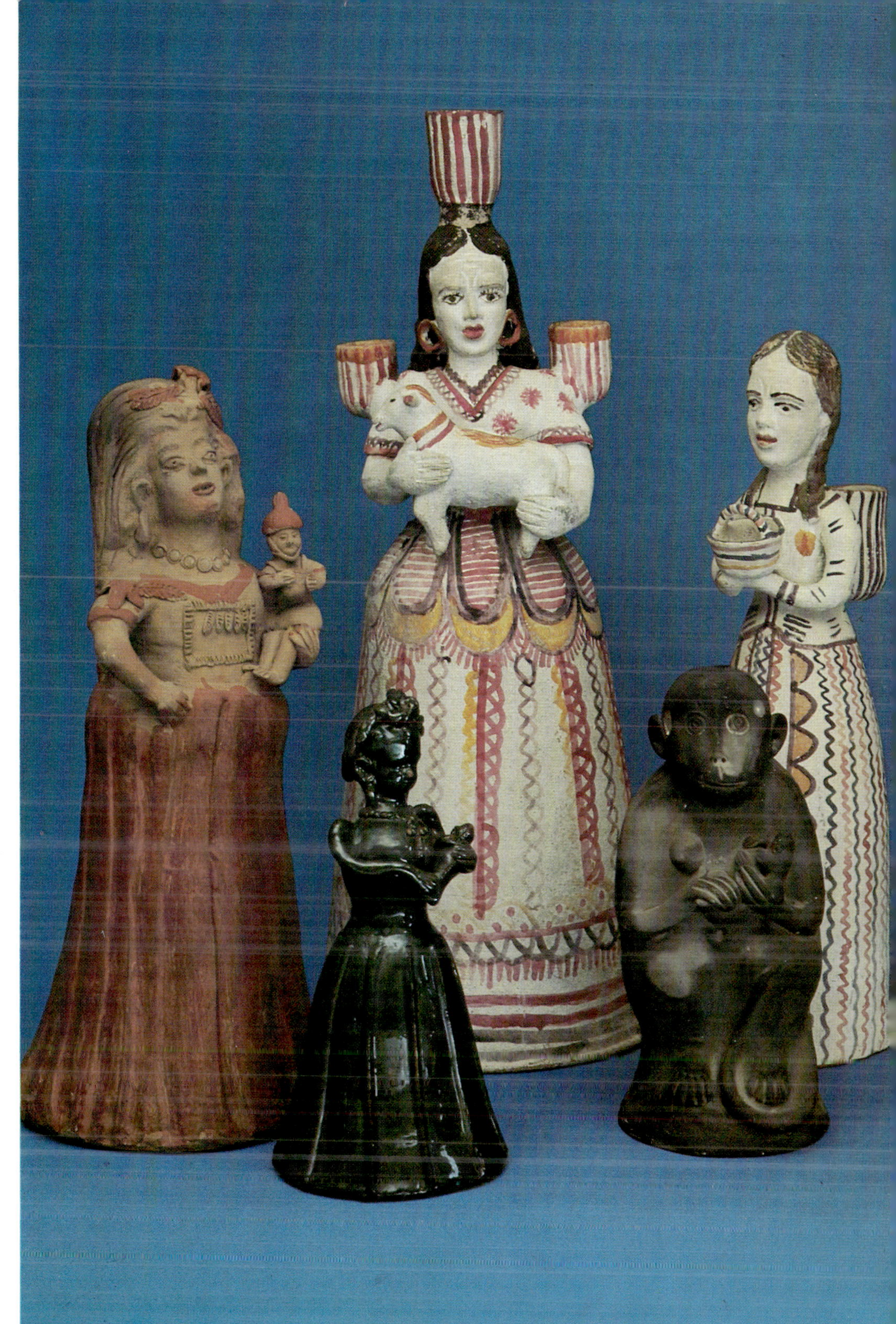

*Holy Family,* by Teodora Blanco, earthenware with appliqued design, Atzompa, State of Oaxaca, Madonna 6″ high. Teodora Blanco is one of the finest and most honored craftswomen of Mexico. Her style of appliqued design is like embroidery that decorates the basic form. In this depiction, Joseph is carrying the lily, and the figures have straw hats slung on their backs, reflecting the actual costume of the region.

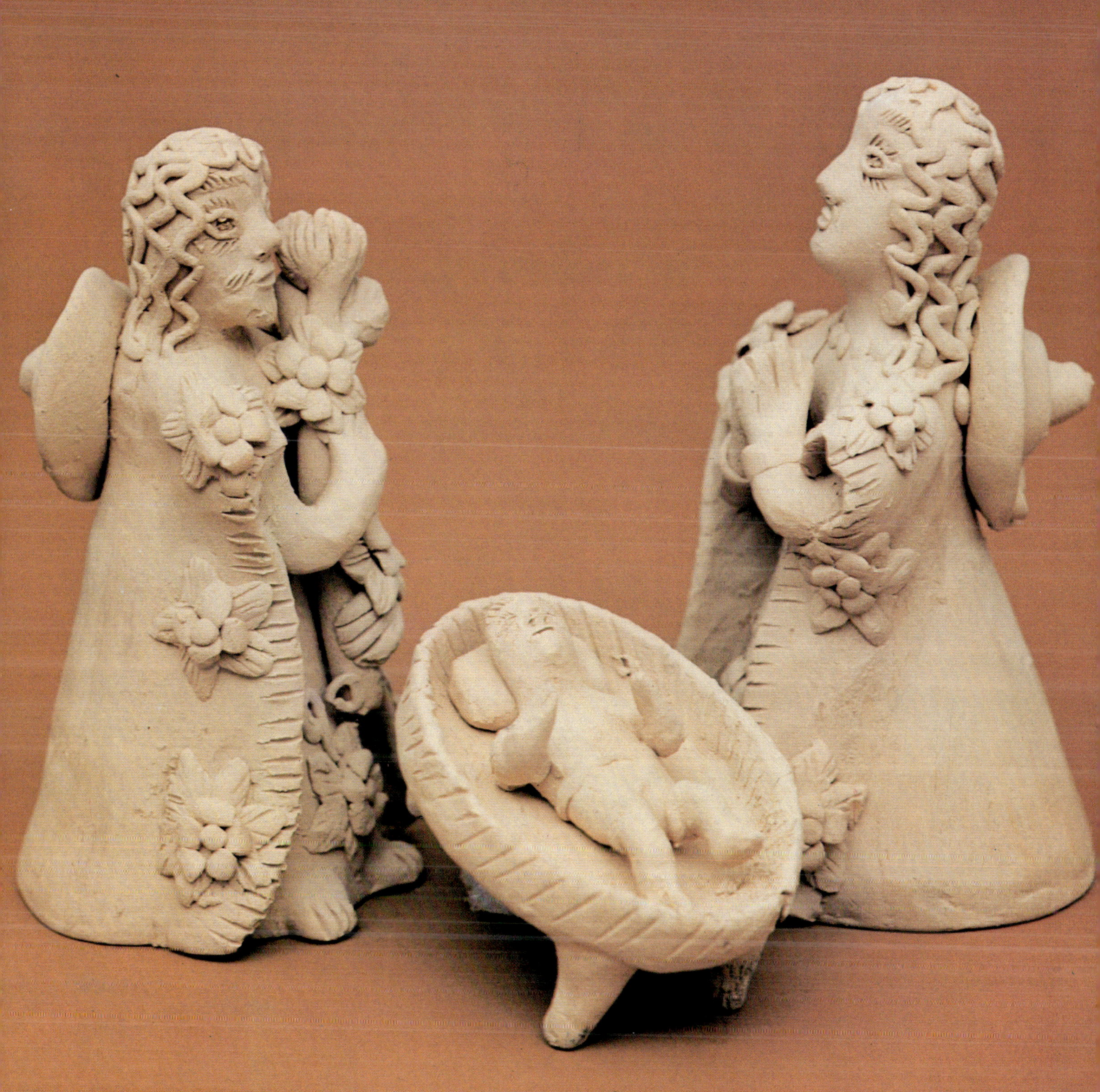

*Mermaid Bottle,* burnished red slip on earthenware with scratched design, Ocotlán, State of Tlaxcala, 10″ high.
*Mermaid,* stained wood with hemp hair, Arrasola, State of Oaxaca, 12″ high.
*Mermaid Bank,* by Candelario Medrano, enameled terra cotta, Santa Cruz, State of Jalisco, 9″ high.
*Mermaid,* enameled terra cotta, Ocumicho, State of Michoacán, 7-1/2″ high.
*Mermaid,* painted terra cotta, Metepec, State of México, 7″ high.

La Sirena, the mermaid, is included in many nativities symbolizing the Goddess of Fertility. Representations of the mermaid are usually found in the highlands where water is not abundant.

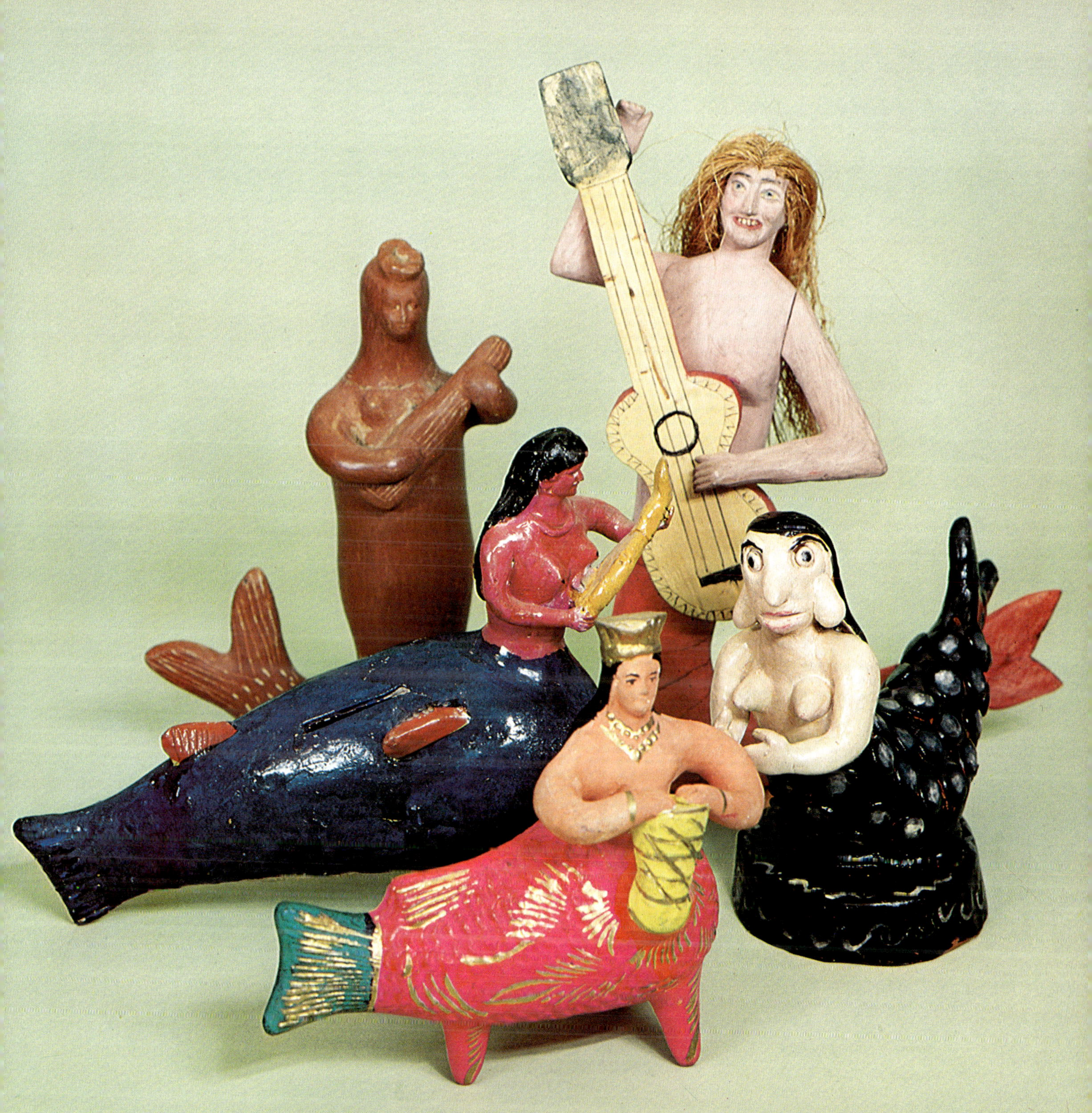

*Mermaid Bottle,* burnished black clay, Coyotepec, State of Oaxaca, 15″ high. Bottles in the mermaid form are made with the belief that the contents are protected. This is a water bottle which is carried by attaching a rope around the waist and around the tail of the bottle and bringing the rope across the carrier's shoulder.

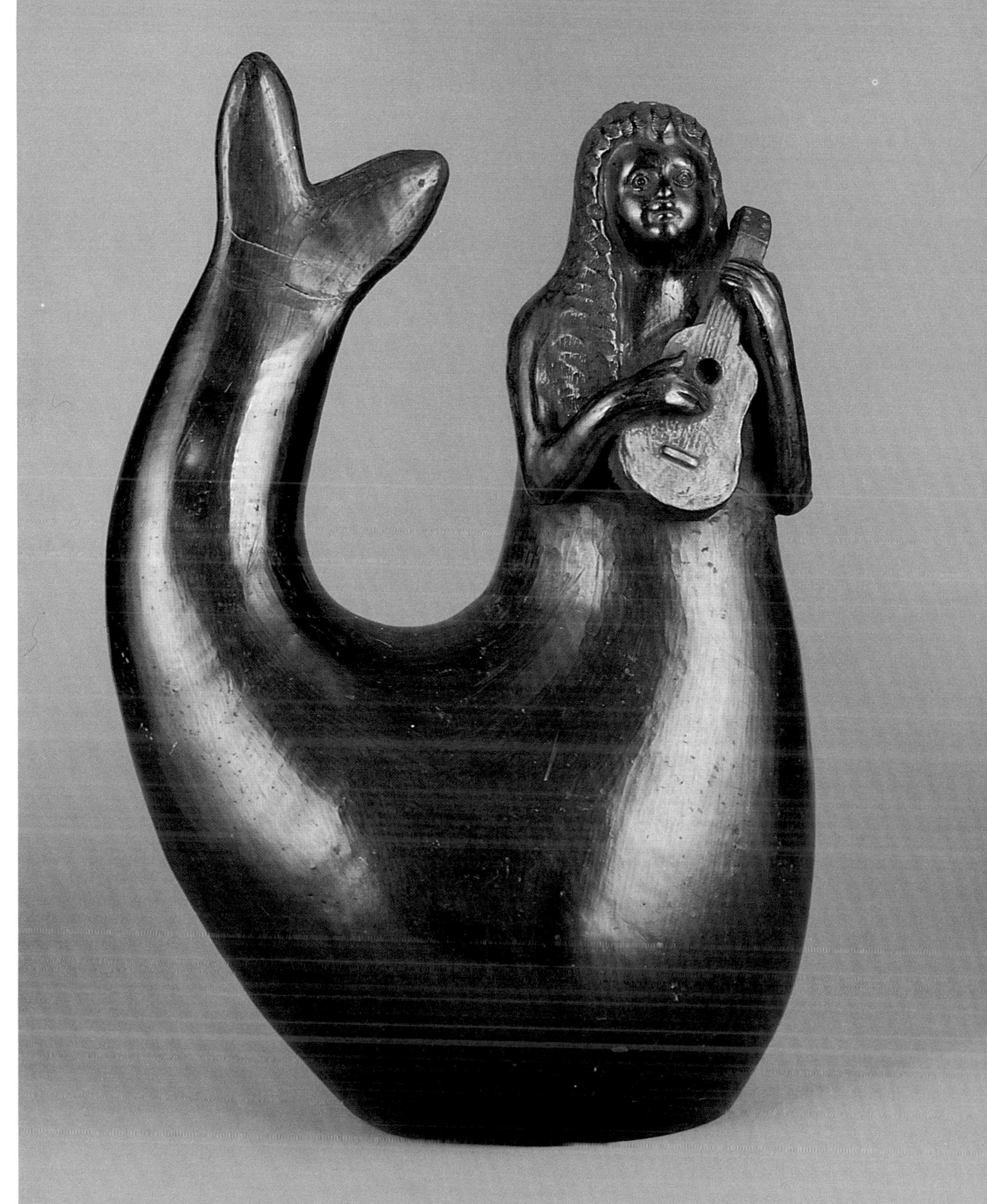

*Nativity*, polychromed and gilded wood, Apaseo el Alto, State of Guanajuato, Madonna 6″ high. Apaseo el Alto has been known for centuries as a center of religious sculpture for the church.

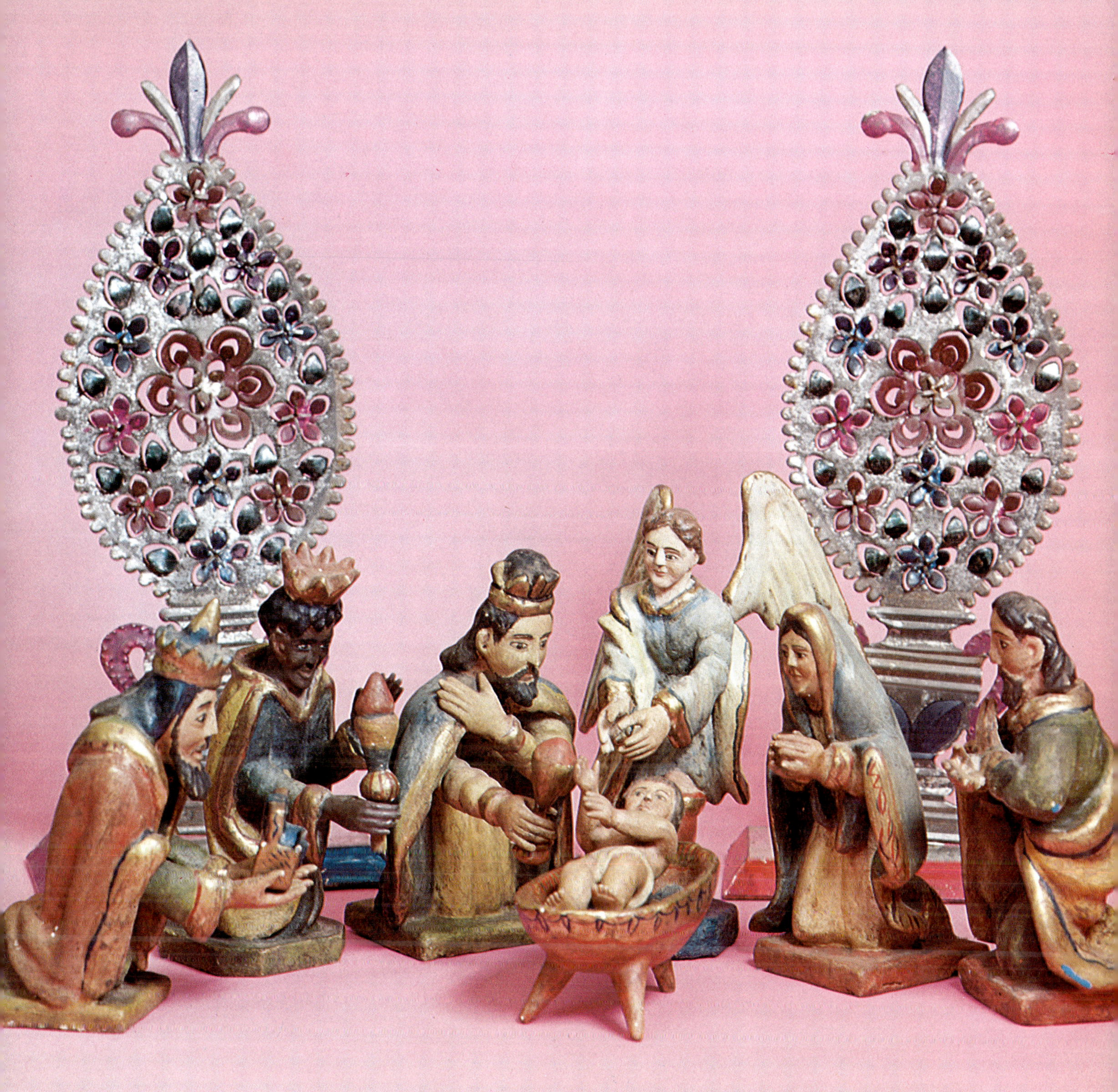

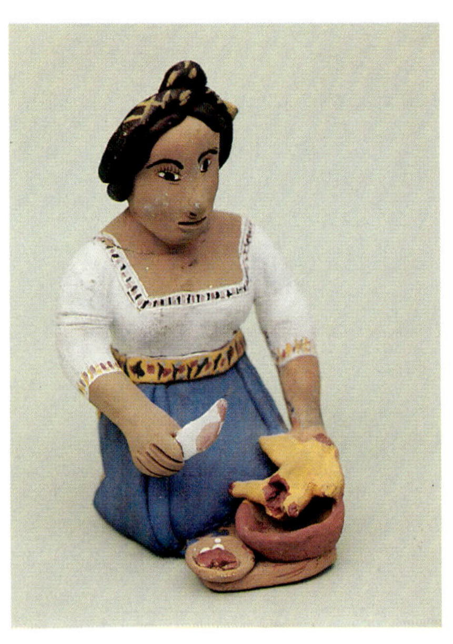

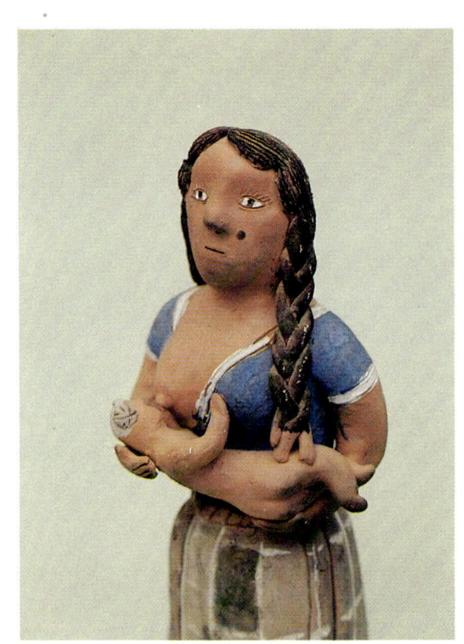

*Nativity*, painted terra cotta, Ocotlán, State of Oaxaca, Madonna 12″ high. This nativity shows the figures bringing gifts in tribute, and it relates everyday happenings to the event. The woman in the foreground is dressing a chicken (see detail) and the woman with child seems to be sharing her own experience with the Madonna (see detail). The small animals around the sensuous mermaid are musicians. The clothing of the figures depict the costumes of the different areas of the State of Oaxaca.

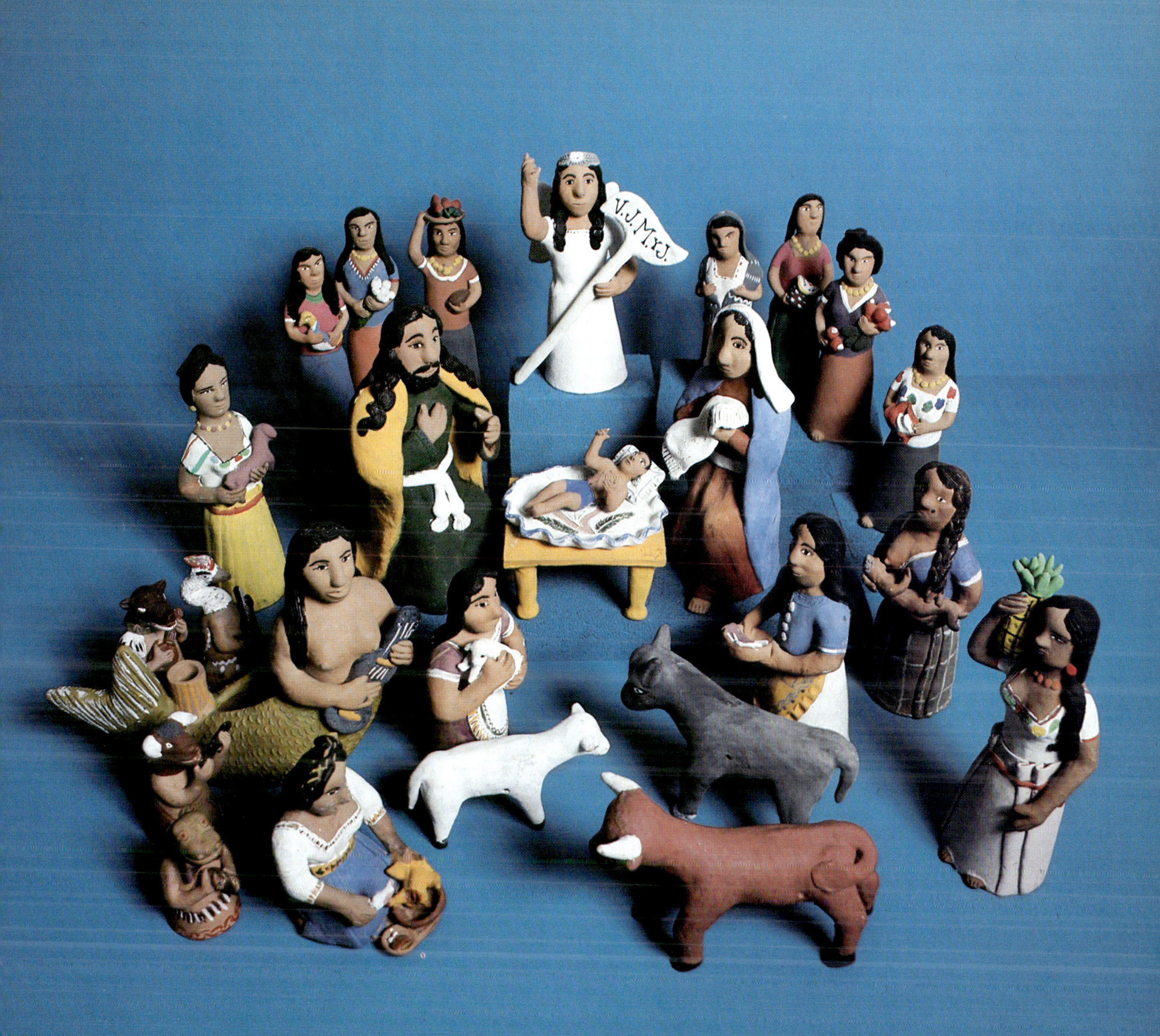
V.J.M.y.J.

*Nativity Candelabra,* painted terra cotta, Metepec, State of México, 23″ high.
The faded colors indicate that this piece is about twenty years old.

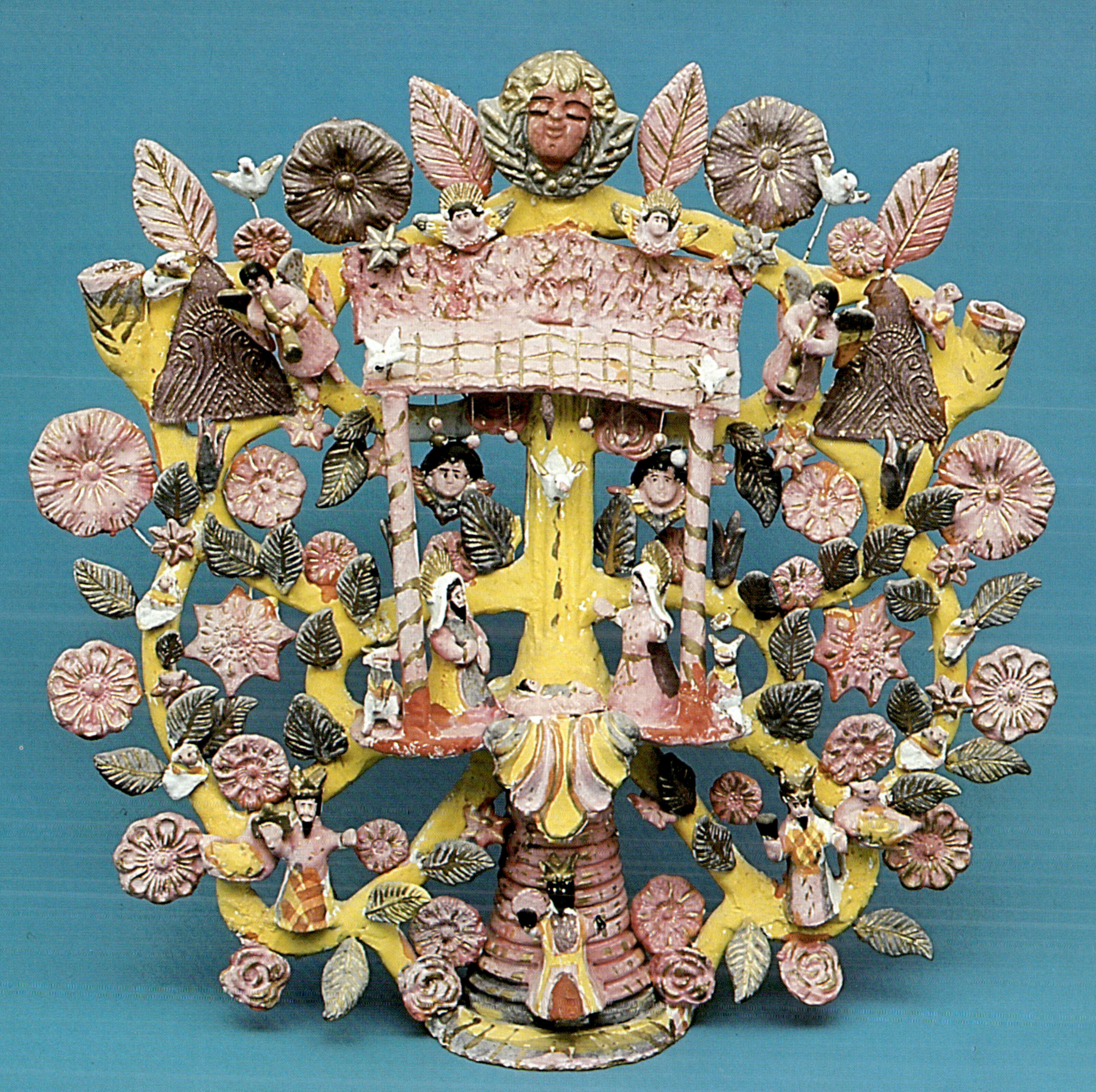

*Lamb of God,* by Jorje Wilmot, painted terra cotta, Monterrey, State of Nueva León, 31-1/2″ high. Wilmot is one of the finest ceramic artists in stoneware in Mexico.
*Nativity,* enameled terra cotta, State of Oaxaca.

The lamb is often used as a seat for the baby Jesus.

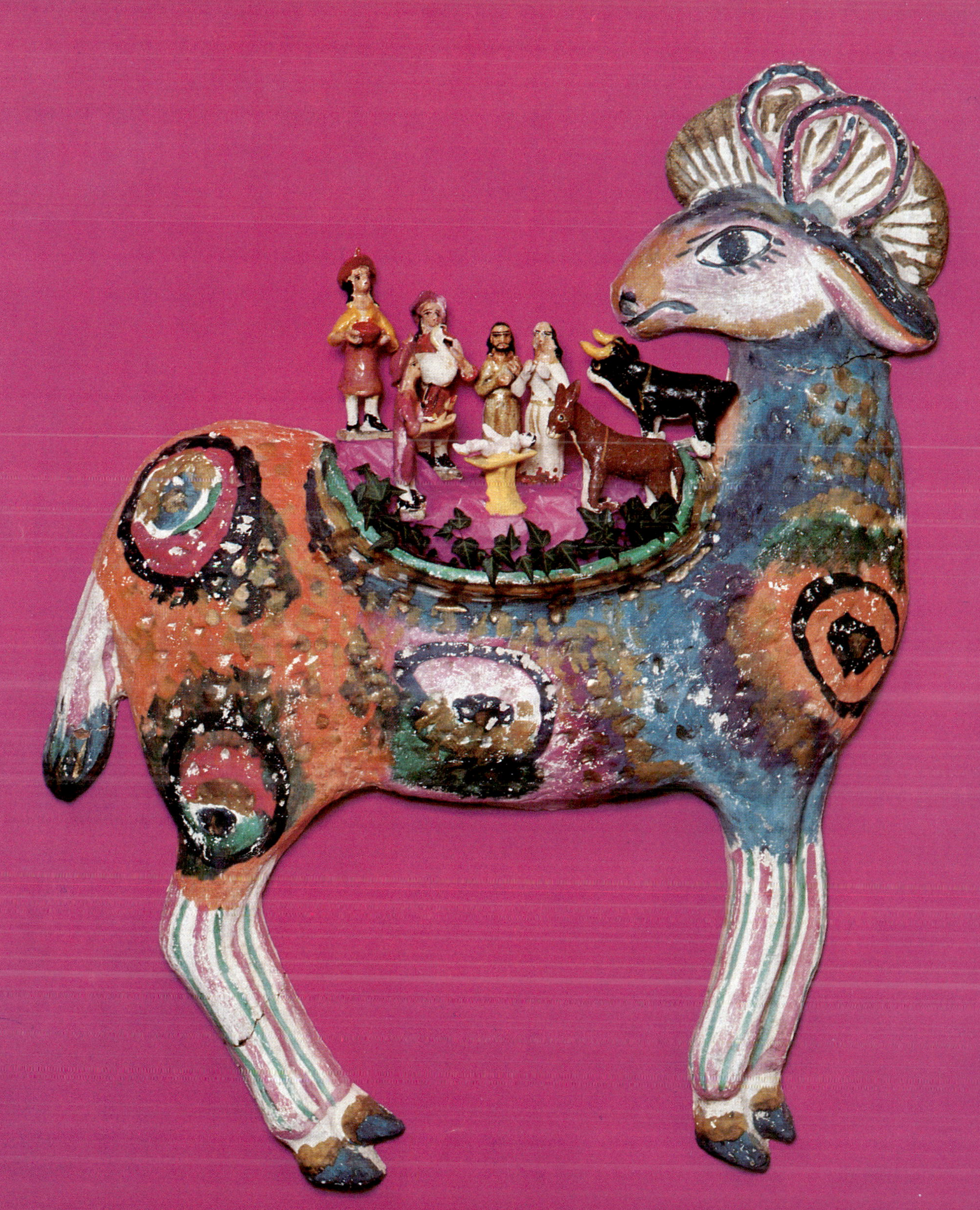

*Adam and Eve Candelabra,* painted terra cotta, Metepec, State of México, 20″ high. Figures of Adam and Eve are much in evidence during the Christmas season; these figures represent a primitive conception which symbolizes the birth of Jesus as the beginning of time.

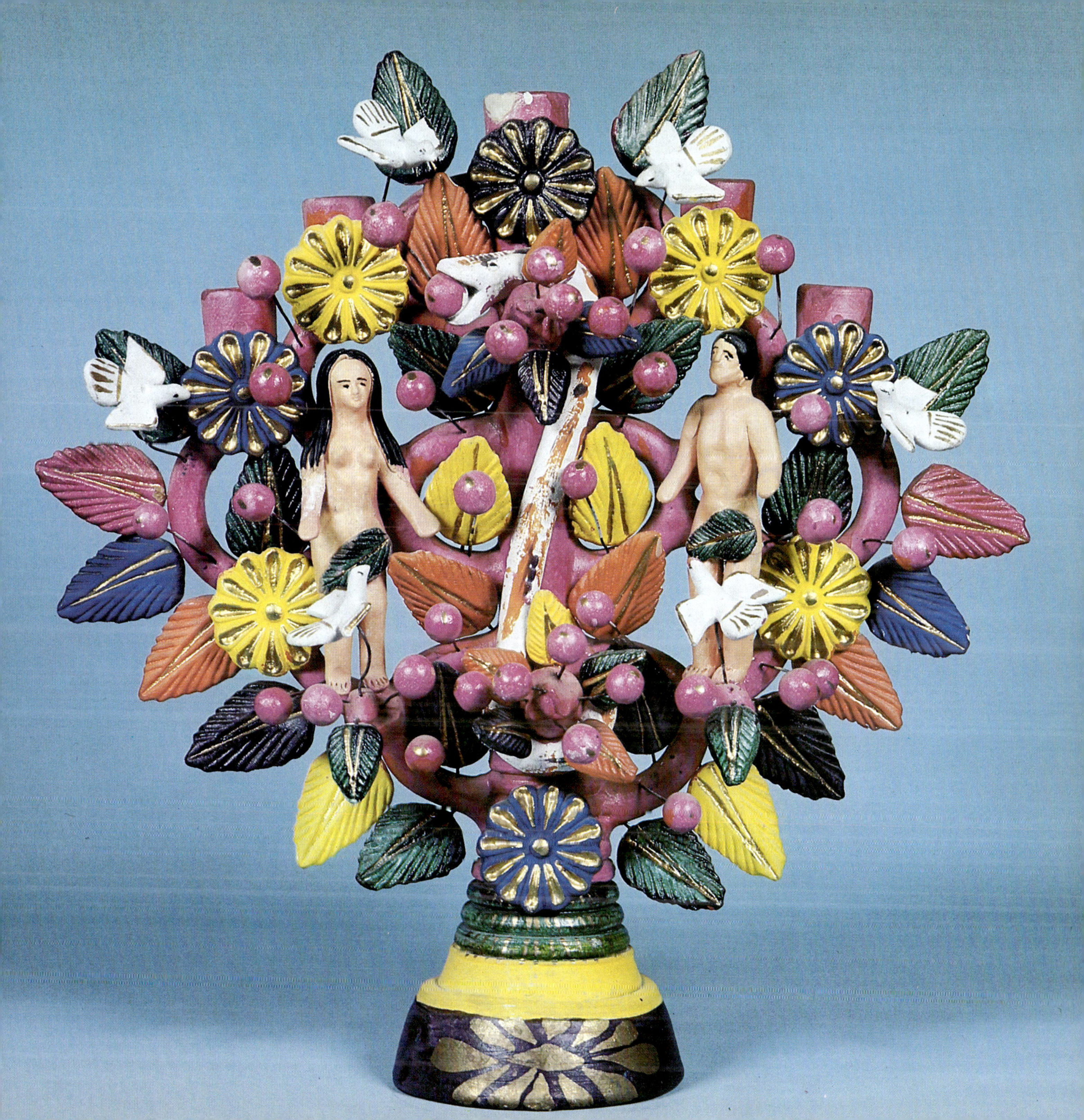

*Adam and Eve,* enameled terra cotta, Ocumicho, State of Michoacán, 8″ high.
*Adam and Eve,* painted earthenware, Acatlán, State of Puebla, 12″ high.
*Adam and Eve,* painted terra cotta, Tlaquepaque, State of Jalisco, 4-1/2″ high.
*Adam and Eve,* painted terra cotta, Metepec, State of México, 6″ high.

These are ornaments to be used in the home as a reminder of the season.

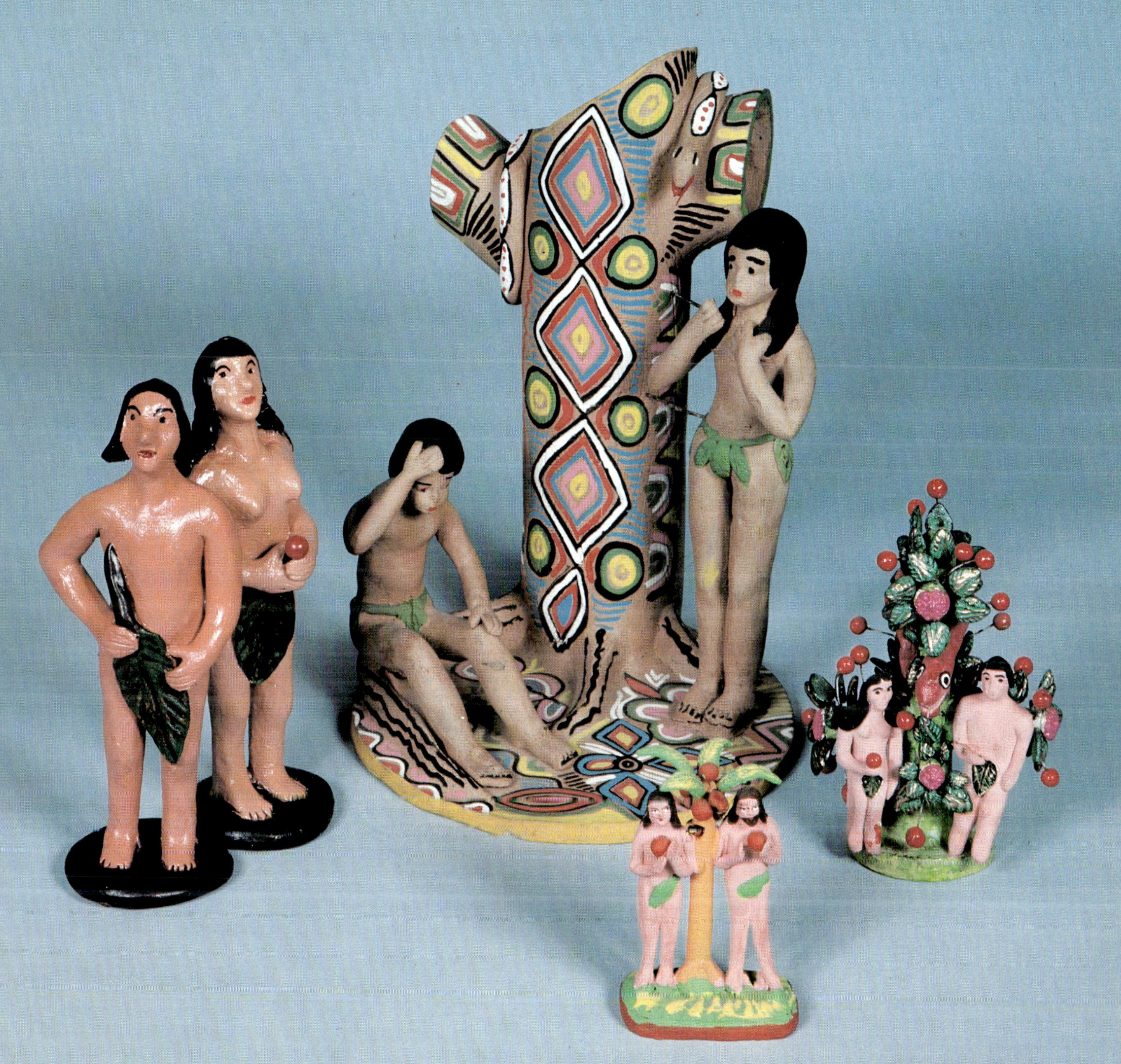

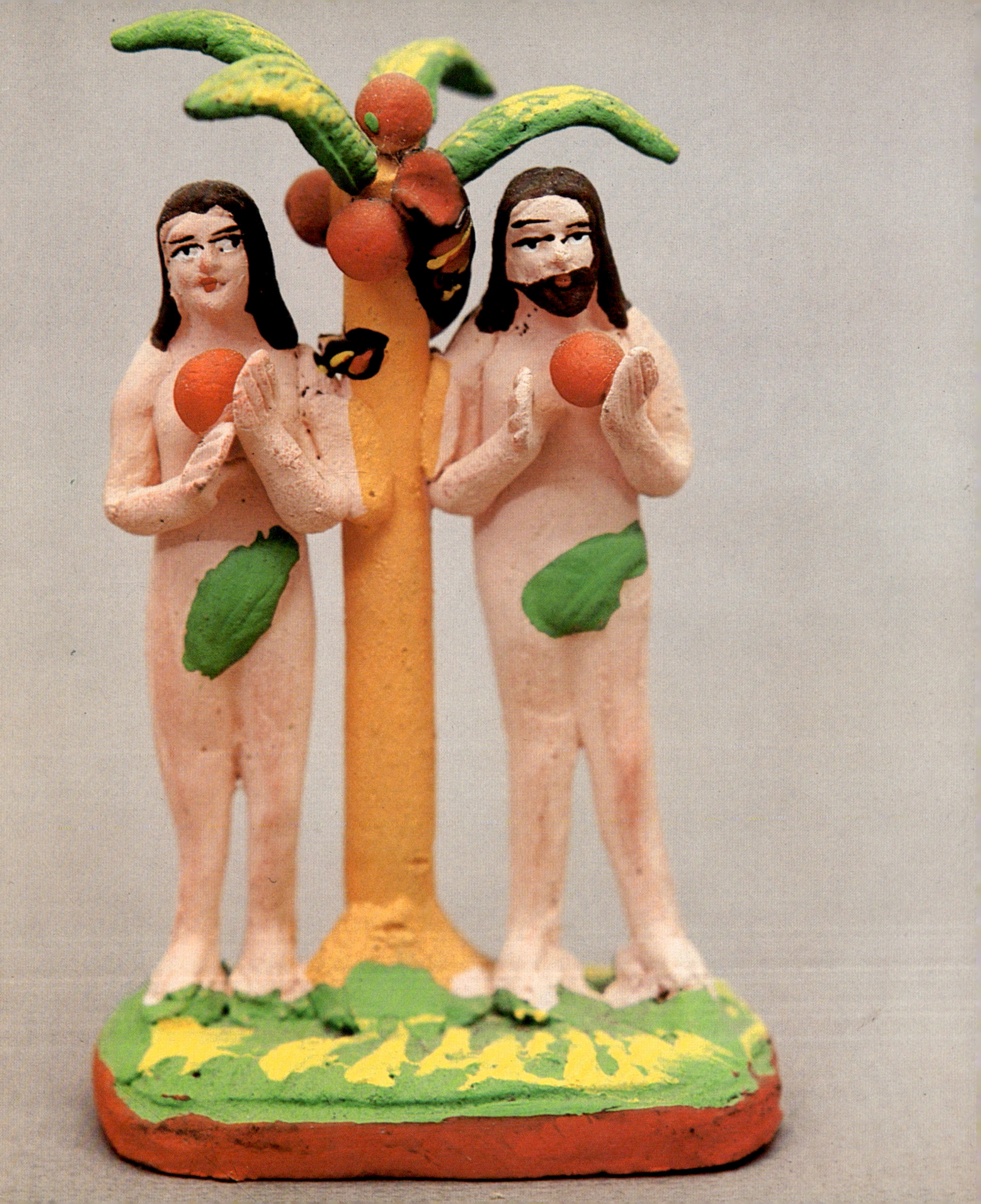

*Adam and Eve*, Tlaquepaque.

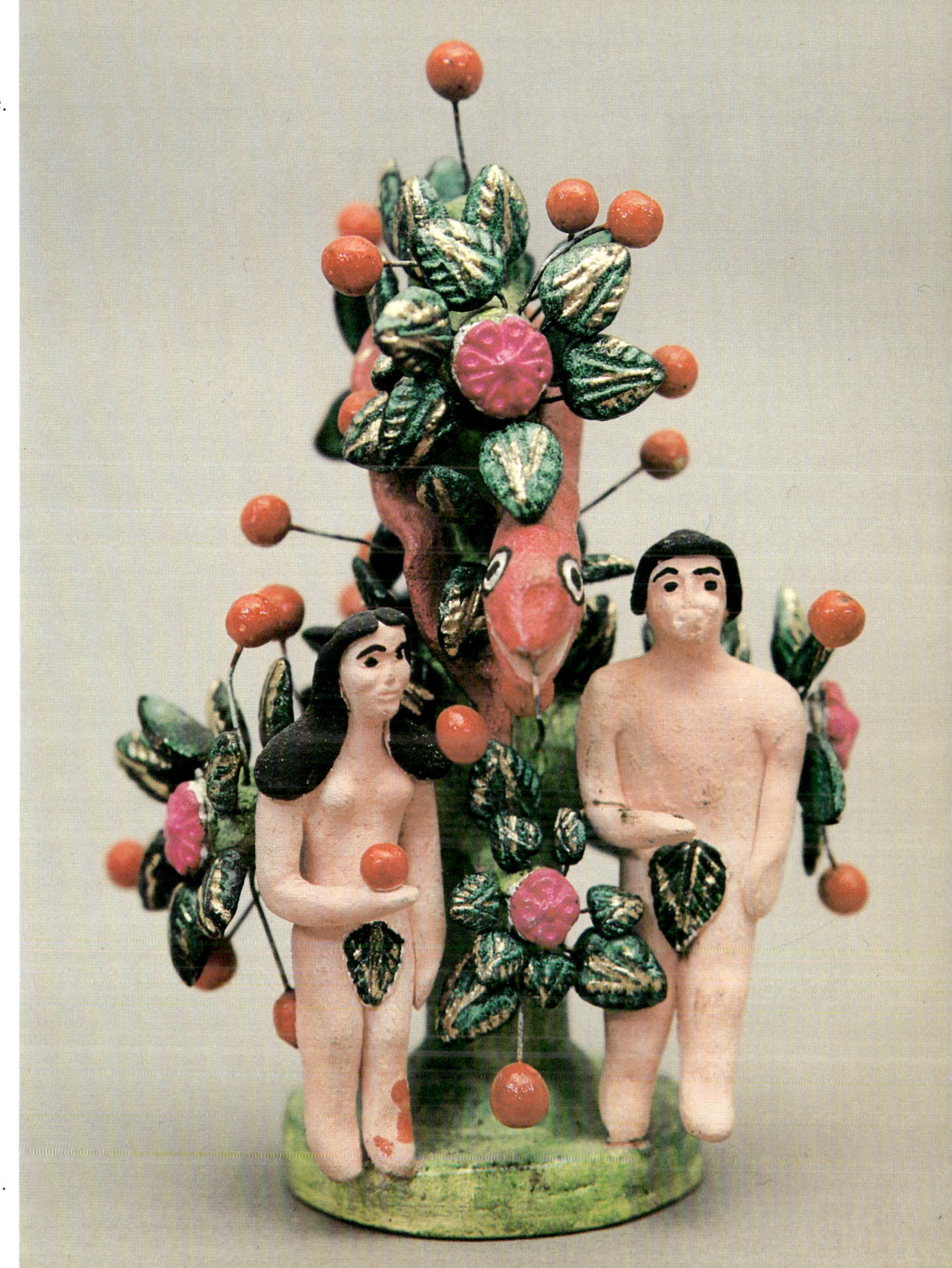

*Adam and Eve*, Metepec.

*Adam and Eve Banner,* detail of cut tissue paper, Puebla, State of Puebla, 13″ high.

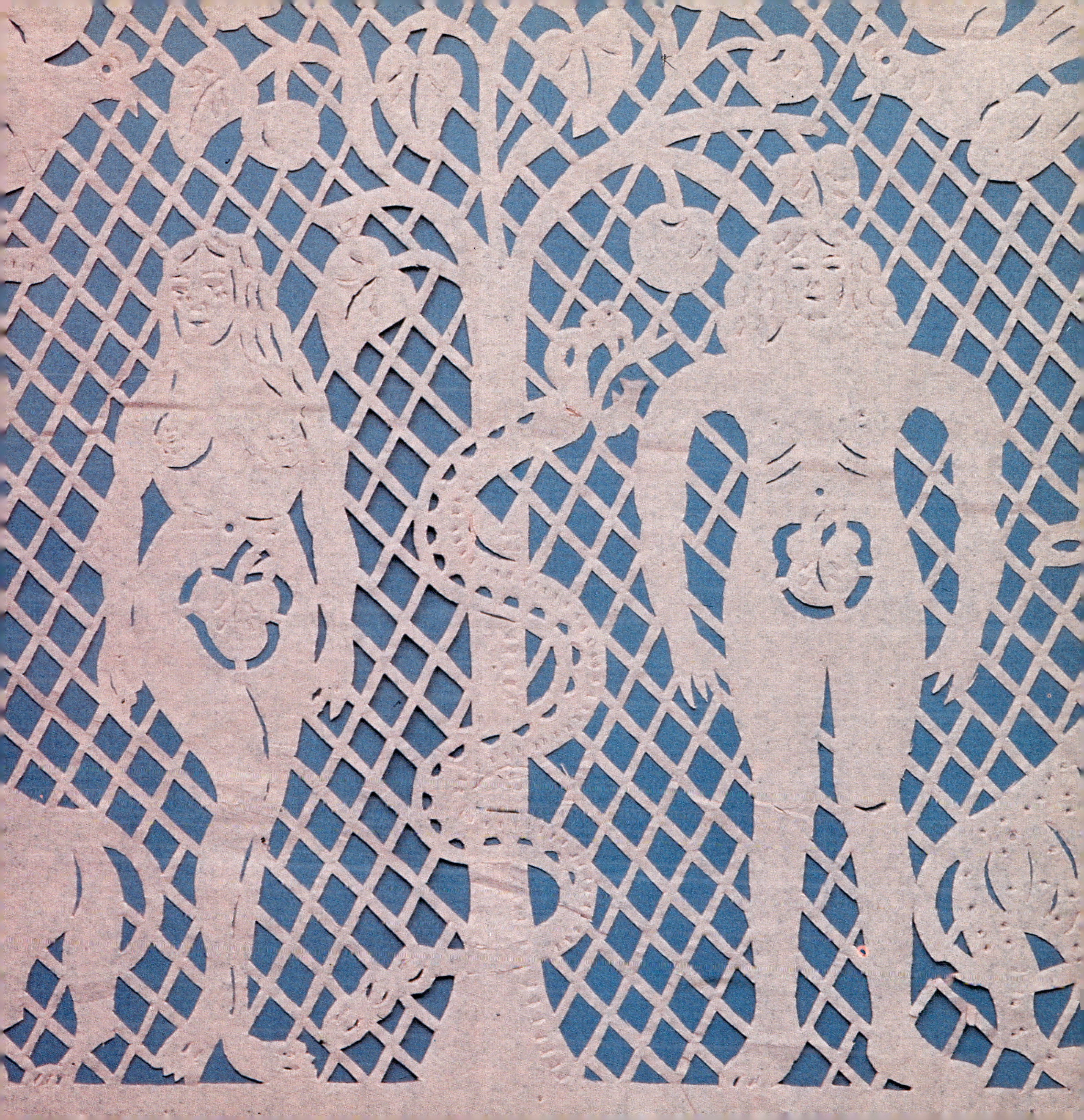

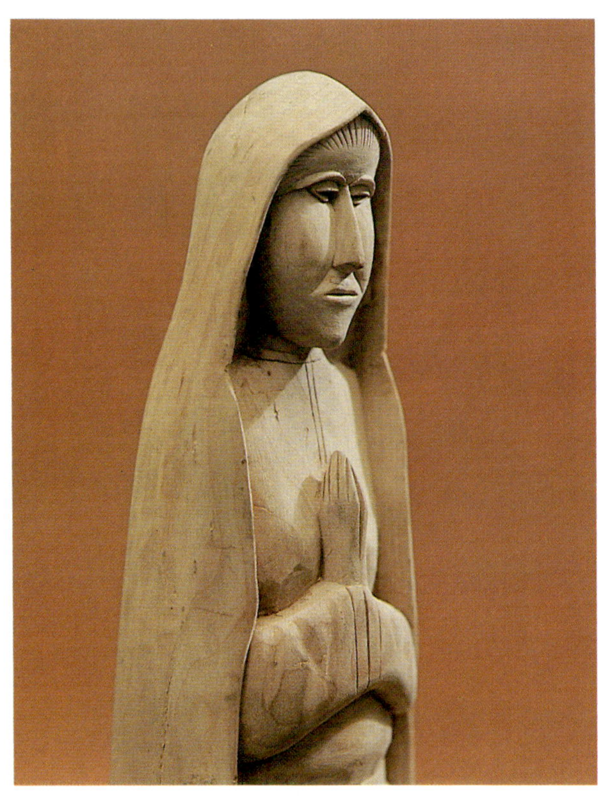

*Madonna,* detail of San Miguel nativity.

*Nativity,* carved cottonwood, San Miguel de Allende, State of Guanajuato, Madonna 13-1/2″ high.

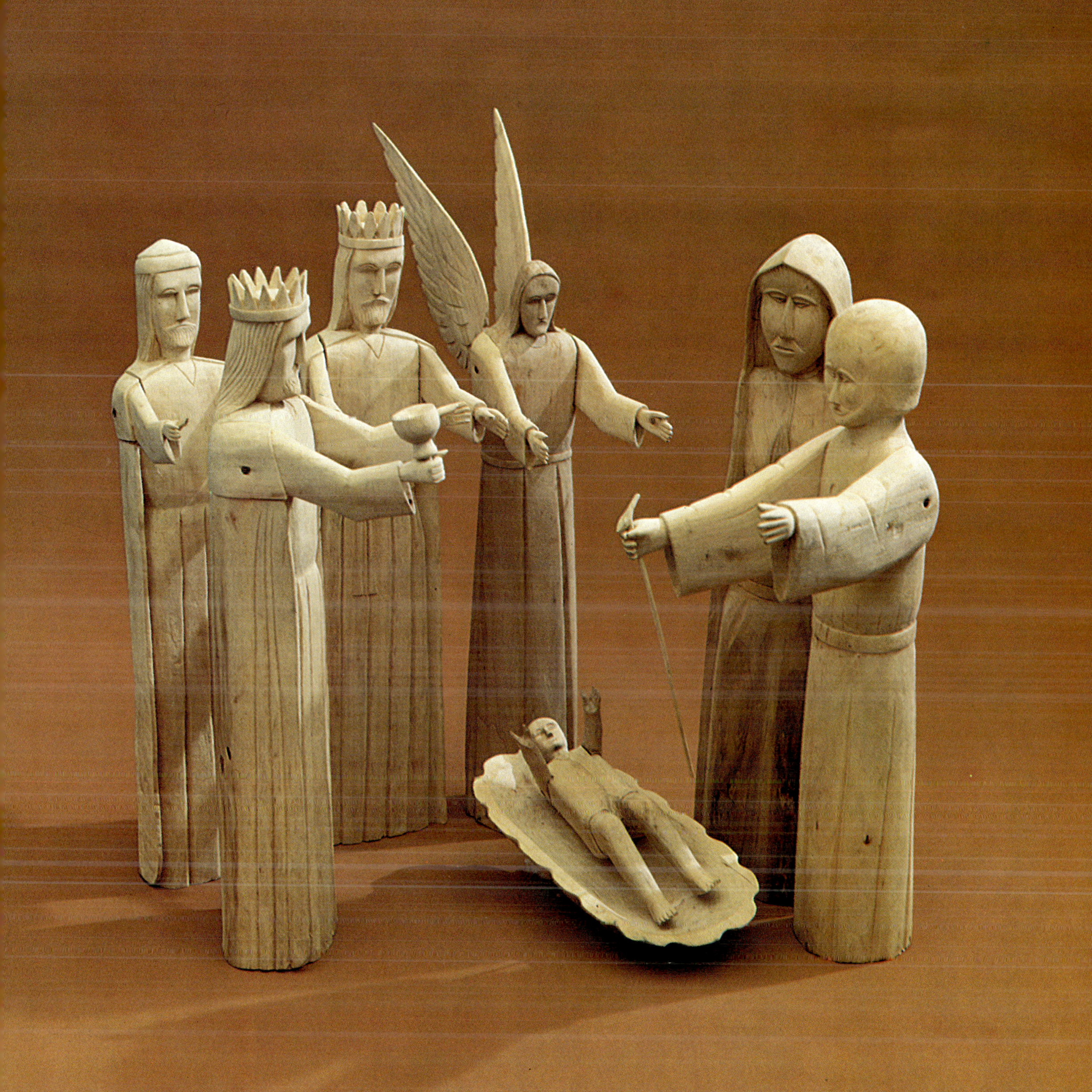

*Nativity,* stained woven palm, Puebla, State of Puebla, figures 3-1/2″ high. Often a band is depicted as if the members were performing for the Christ child.

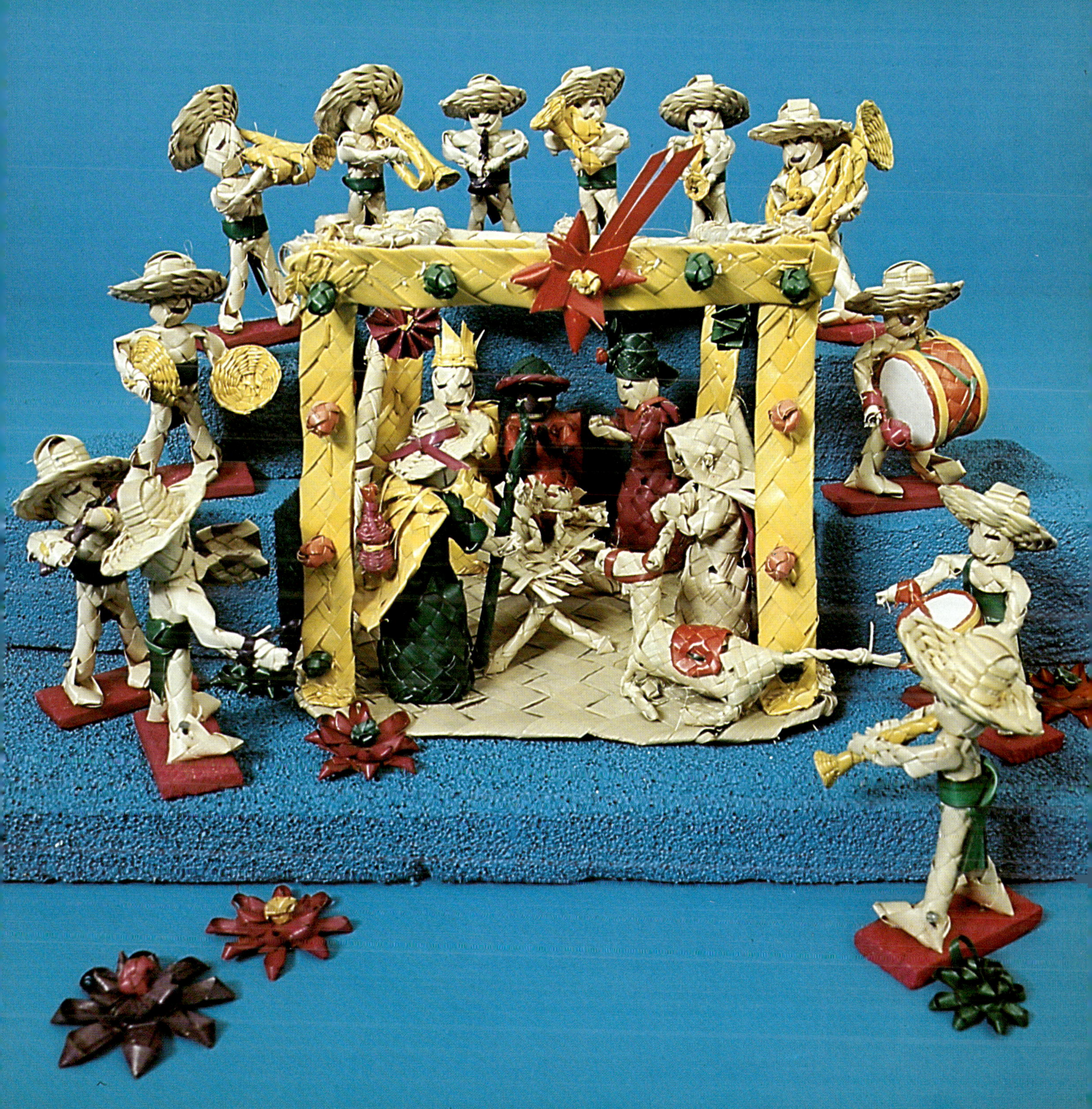

*Nativity*, enameled terra cotta, Ocumicho, State of Michoacán, 12″ high. The size of the child is much too large for the other figures, but, after all, it is his birthday that is celebrated. The child figure is often made purposely large to indicate his importance. Also, the face on the child is sometimes that of an old man, the legend being that the child was born with the sins of the world on his back and that is why he looked like a little old man when he was born.

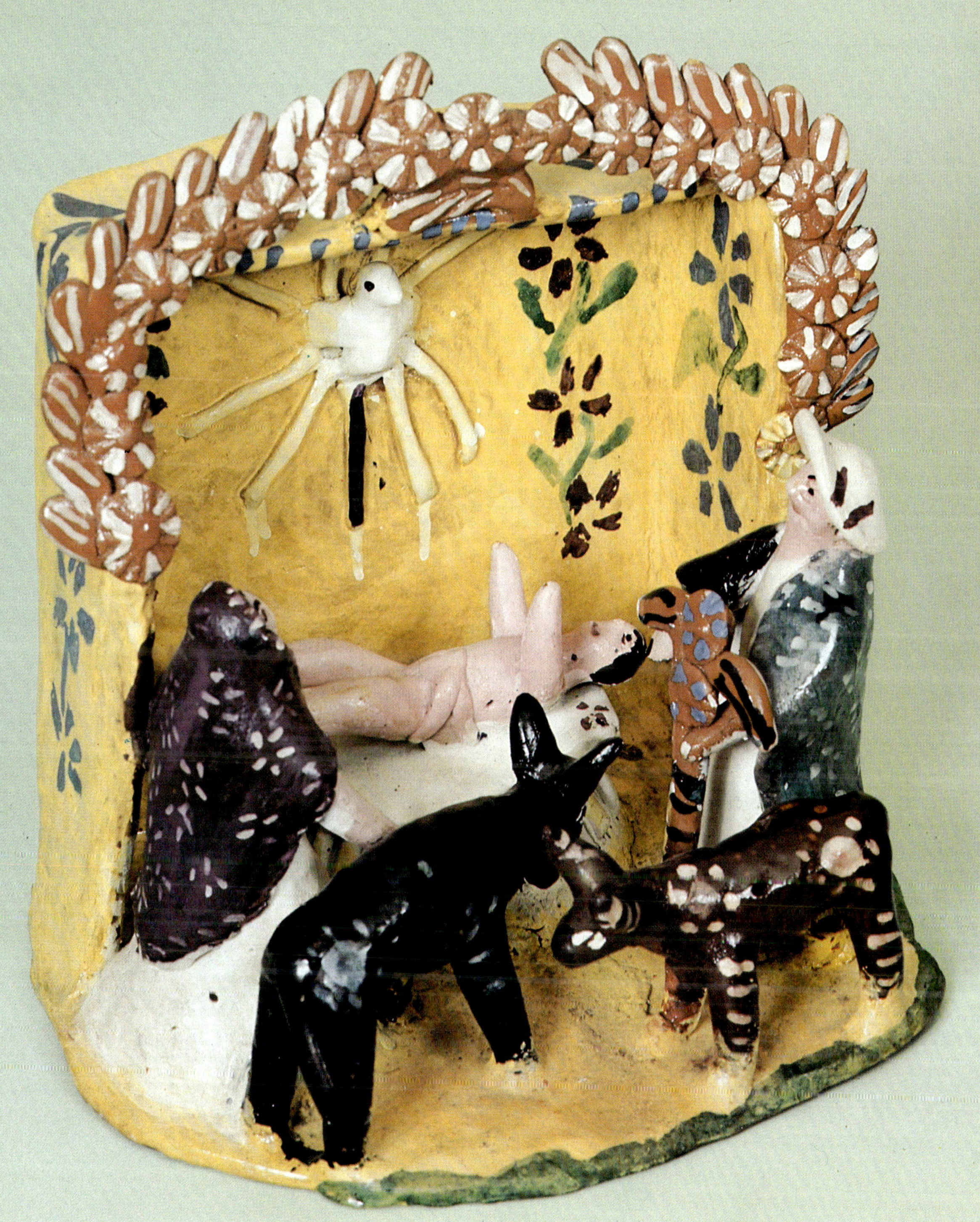

*Nativity,* slip painted and glazed terra cotta, Tzintzuntzan, State of Michoacán, Madonna 7-1/2″ high. This nativity is created in the same manner as the household pottery of the area. There is an abundance of terra cotta clay available in Tzintzuntzan, but to make the figures resemble wheat straw, the terra cotta is slipped with a cream-colored clay which is imported, then glazed, which gives the finished piece the lustre of the wheat straw.

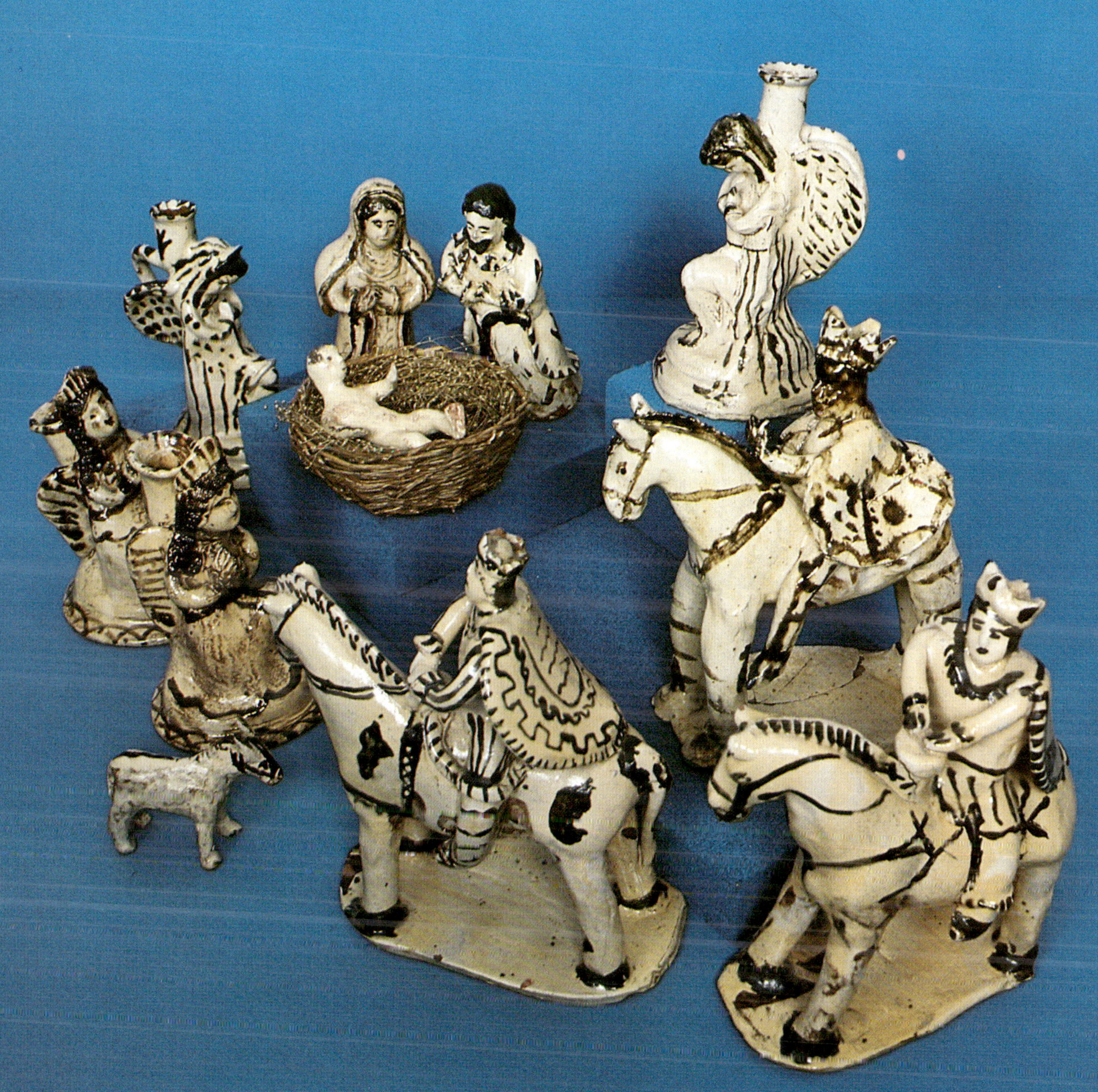

*Nativity*, natural wheat straw, Tzintzuntzan, State of Michoacán, 17″ high.

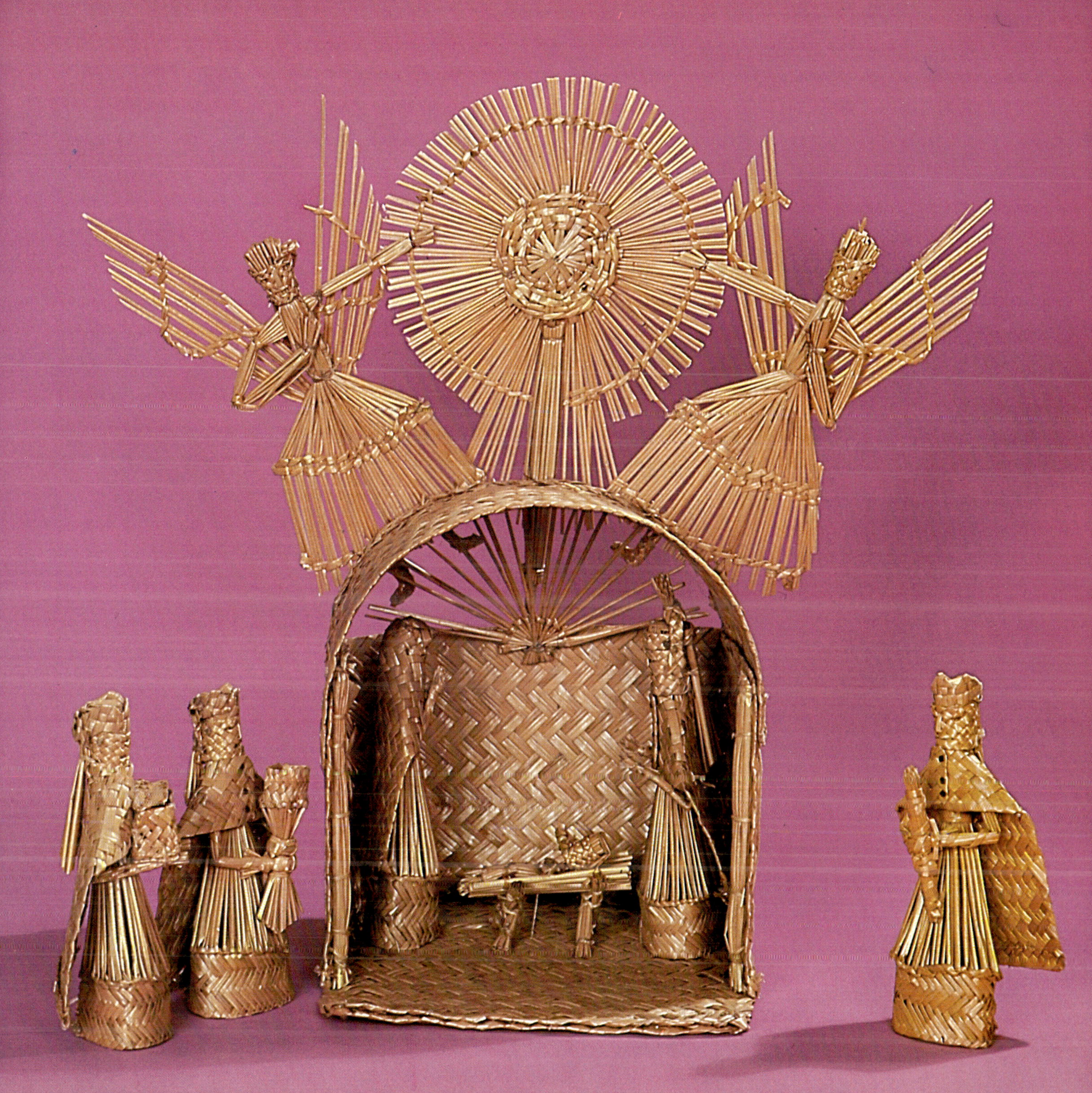

*Nativity,* stained earthenware, Acatlán, State of Puebla, Madonna 5″ high. The Madonna is seated in a chair, an unusual interpretation. The child's head is large, again putting the emphasis on the child rather than on the other figures.

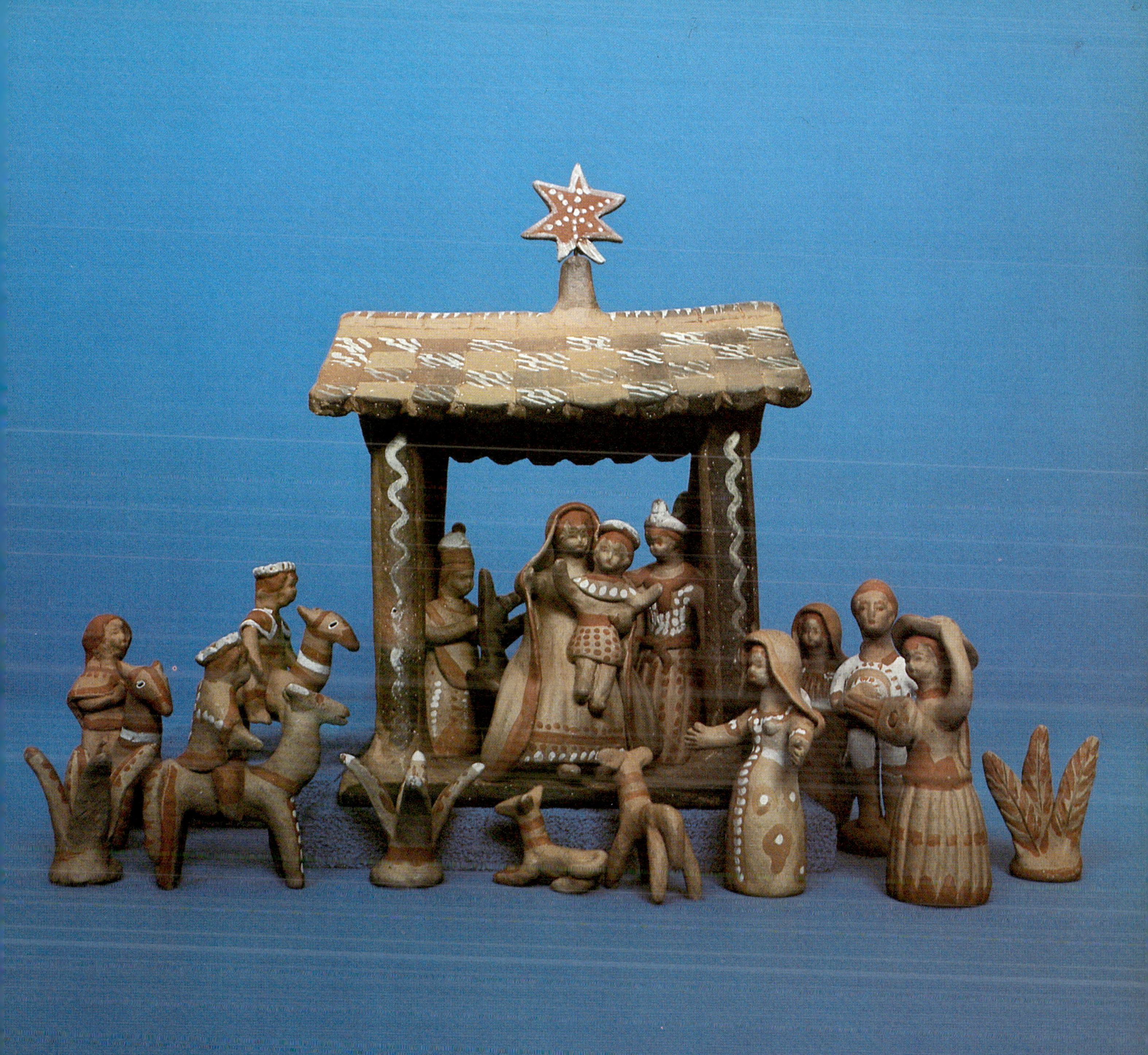

*Nativity,* painted clay, wire, and cardboard, Puebla, State of Puebla or Tlaquepaque, State of Jalisco (miniatures are made in both places and it is difficult to differentiate when purchased in other locations), 3-1/2″ high.
*Toy altar ornaments,* cast lead, Mexico. These lead ornaments were made as toys for the children to create their own altars after having been to church. The ornaments are made in various places around Mexico; the artisans of Mexico take great pleasure in making the miniature toys.

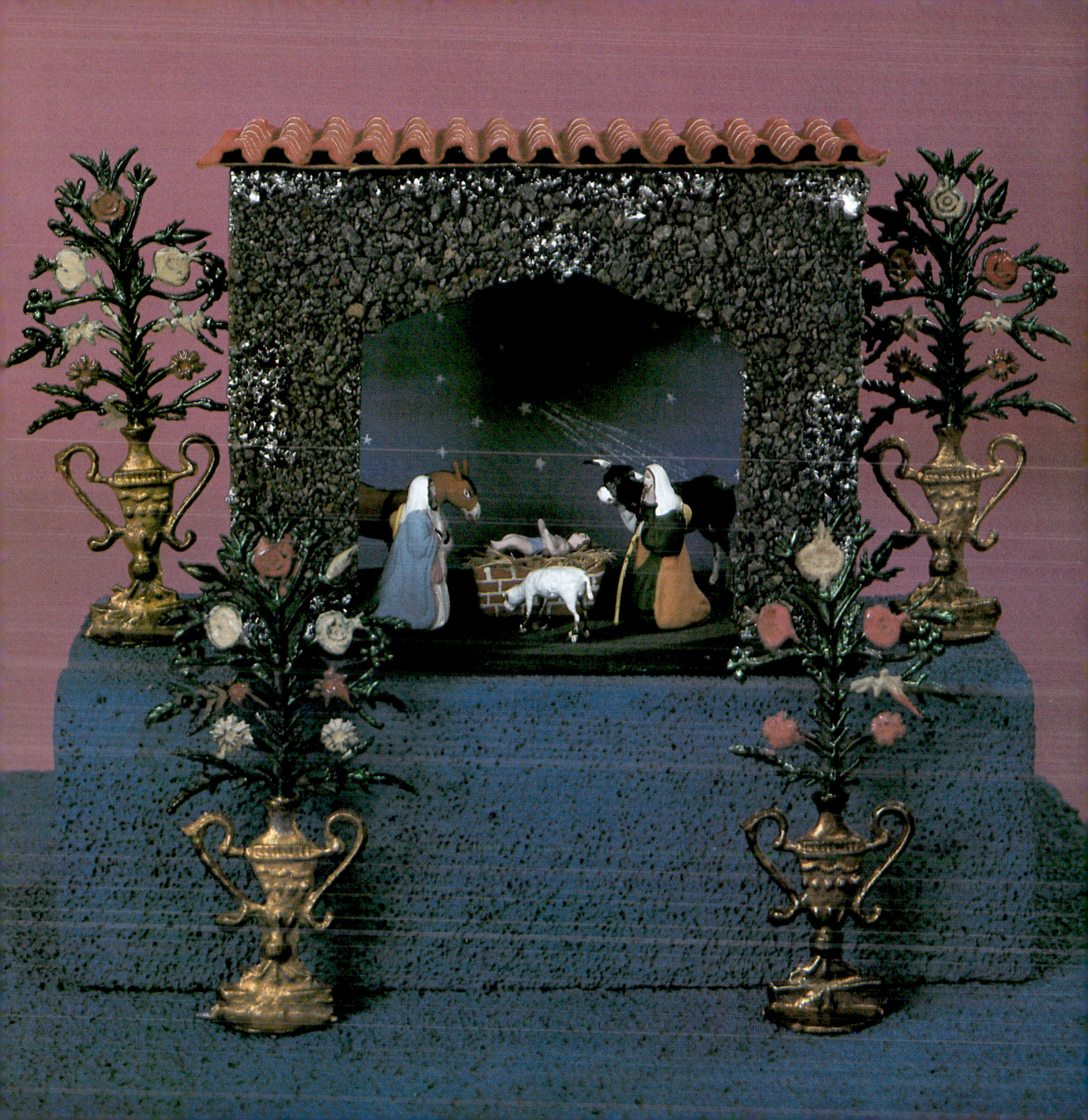

*Nativity,* stained wood and straw, Arrasola, State of Oaxaca, 20″ high. The doors of this piece can be closed and possibly were kept closed until Christmas Eve.

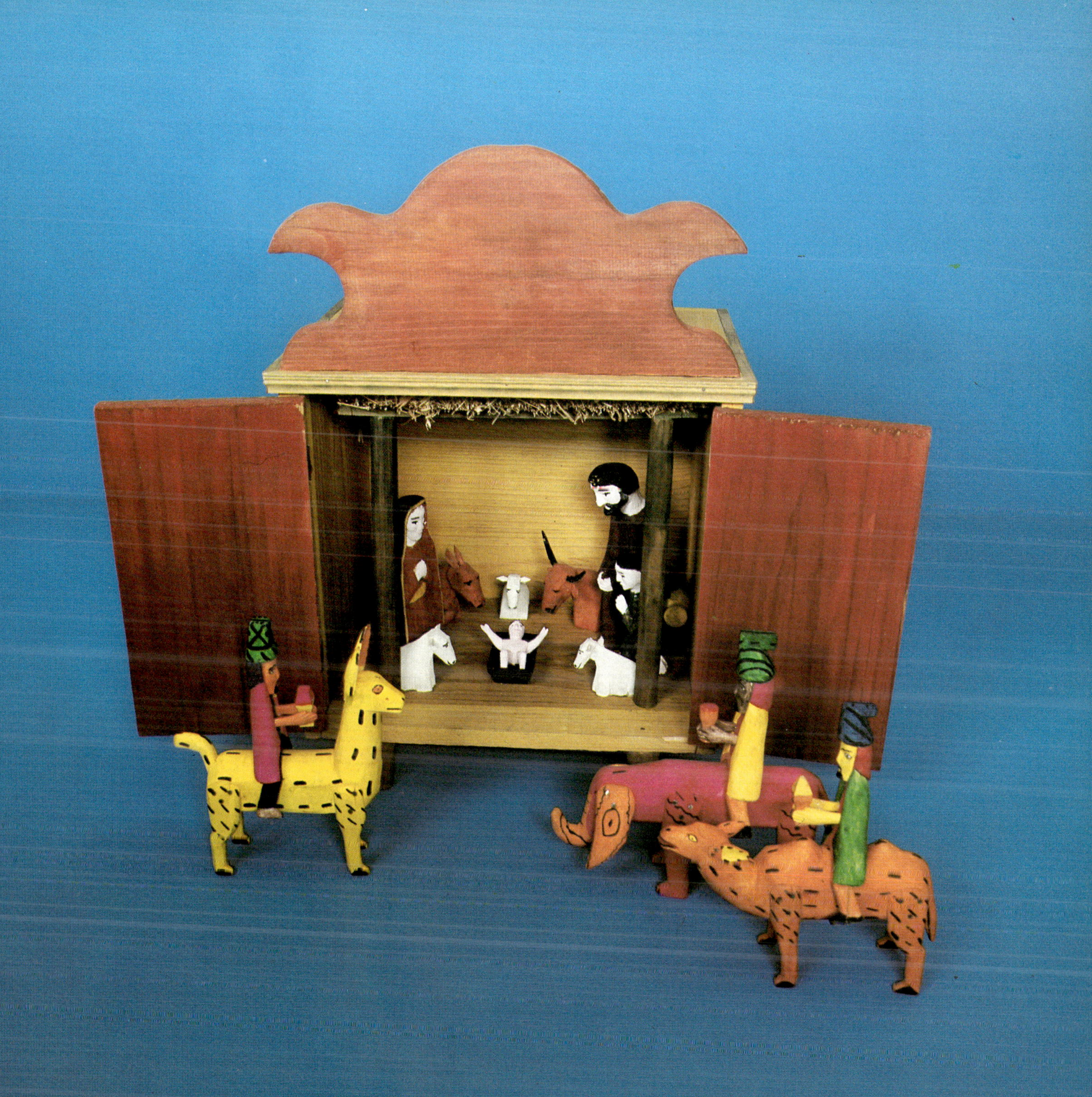

# V.J.M.y J.

*December 26*

Los Pastores. The presentation of the miracle play.

*Los Pastores Masks*
*Bull,* by Candelario Medrano, enameled terra cotta, Santa Cruz, State of Jalisco, 8″ high.
*Cat,* painted wood, Olinalá, State of Guerrero, 14-1/2″ high.
*Dog,* painted wood, Colonial, 14″ high.
*Devil,* enameled wood with horn, hair and leather, Olinalá, State of Guerrero, 13″ high.
*Shepherd,* painted wood, Colonial, 9″ high.
*Devil,* enameled tin, Saltillo, State of Coahuila, 12-1/2″ high.
*Shepherdess,* painted wood, Colonial, 7″ high.
*Old Man,* papier mache and hemp, Celaya, State of Guanajuato, face 9″ high.
*Shepherd,* painted wood, Colonial, 10″ high.

The masks are made to be worn by the players in the miracle play. The interpretation of Los Pastores varies in different regions of Mexico, and many of the plays include additional characters such as animals.

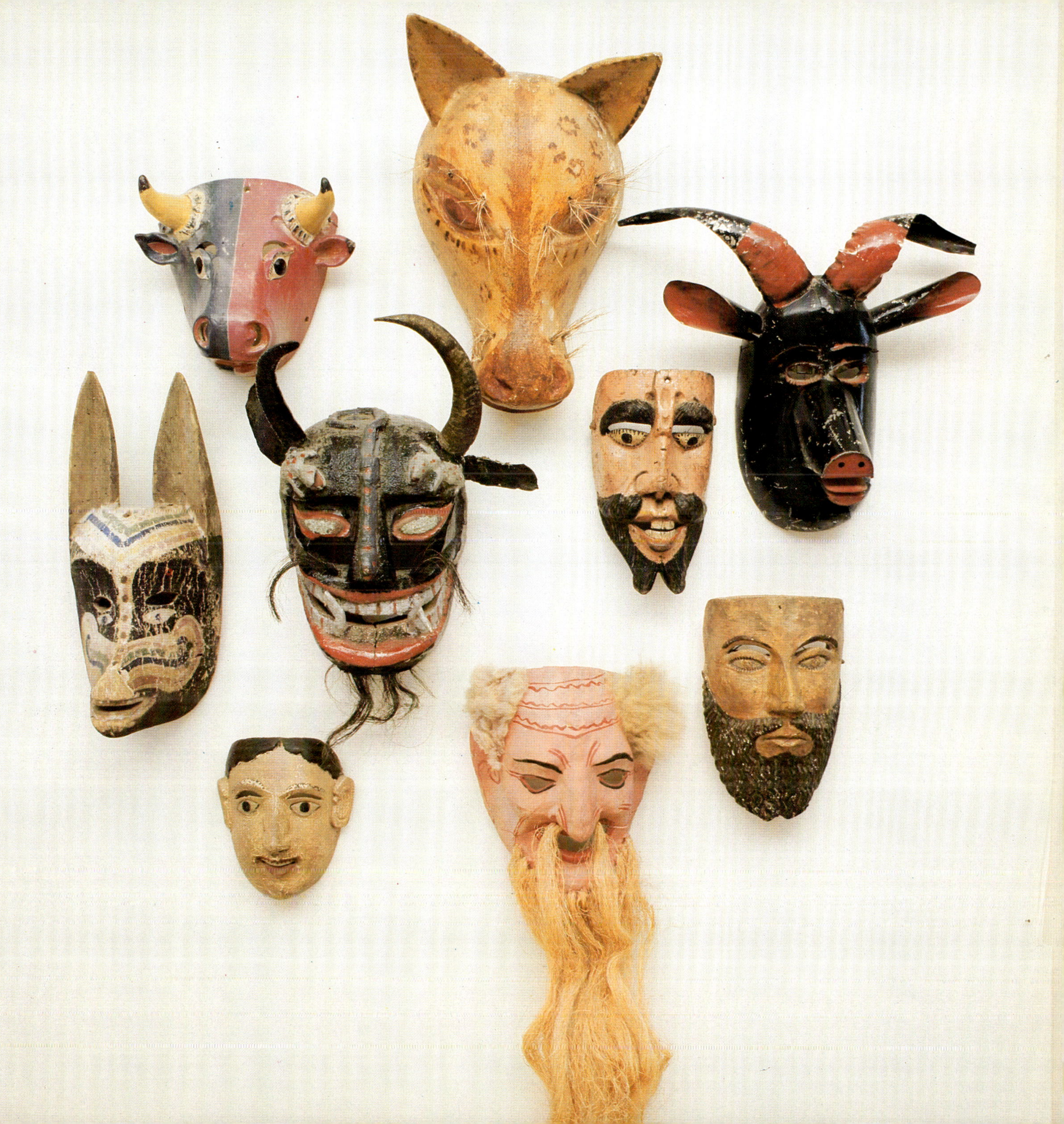

# V.J.M.y J.

*January 6*
El Día de los Santos Reyes. The day of gift-giving.

*Three Kings,* by Candelario Medrano, enameled terra cotta, Santa Cruz, State of Jalisco, 6-1/2″ high. The horses are very much like the tomb ceramics of ancient China.

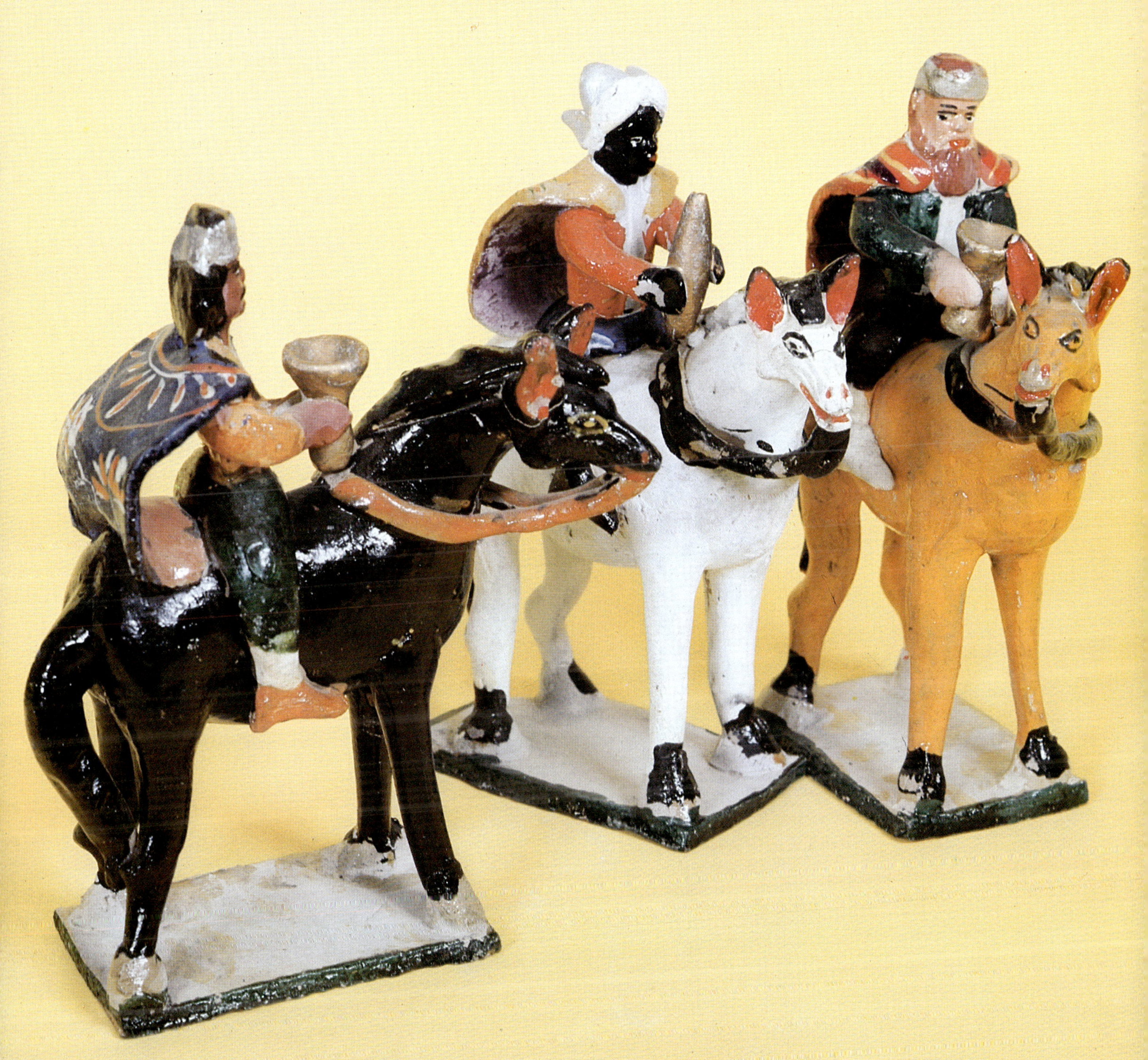

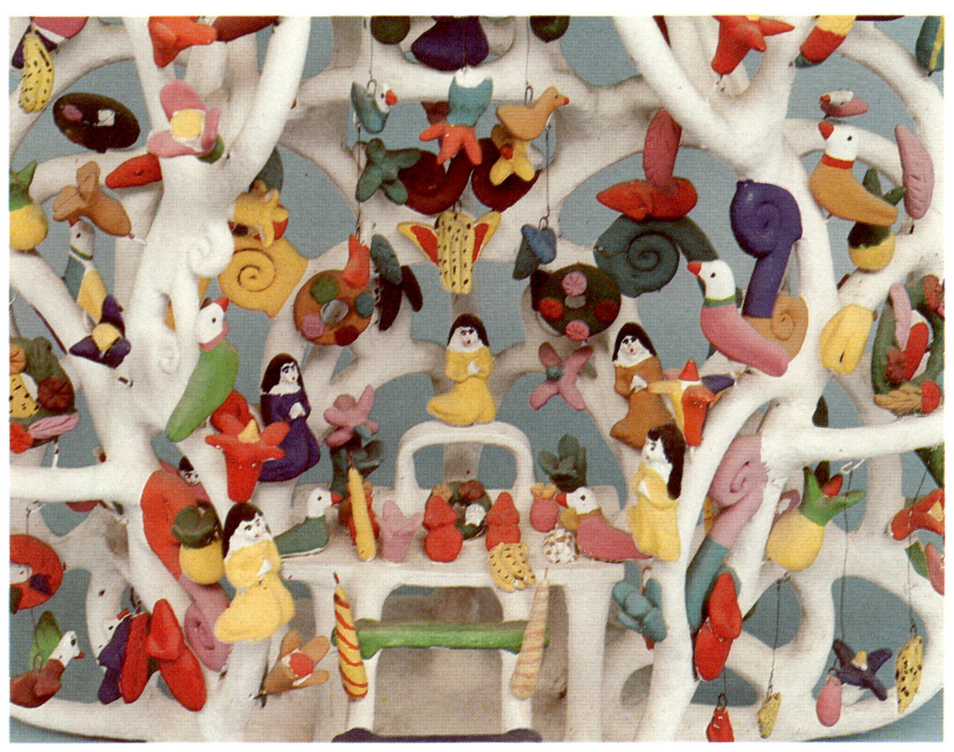

*Altar Piece for the Day of the Kings*, painted earthenware, Acatlán, State of Puebla, 55″ high. Special breads in many shapes are placed on the altar for blessing on this day.

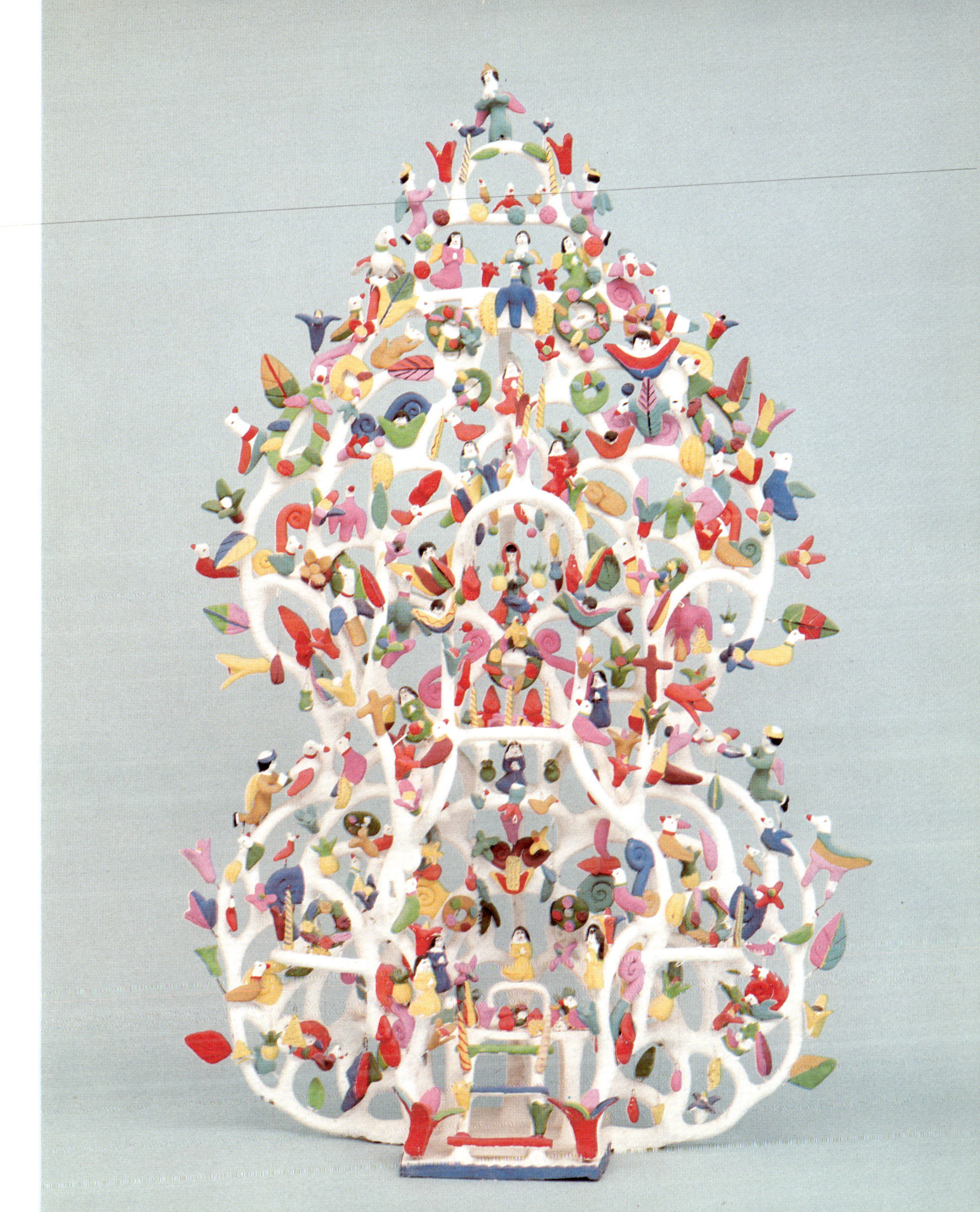

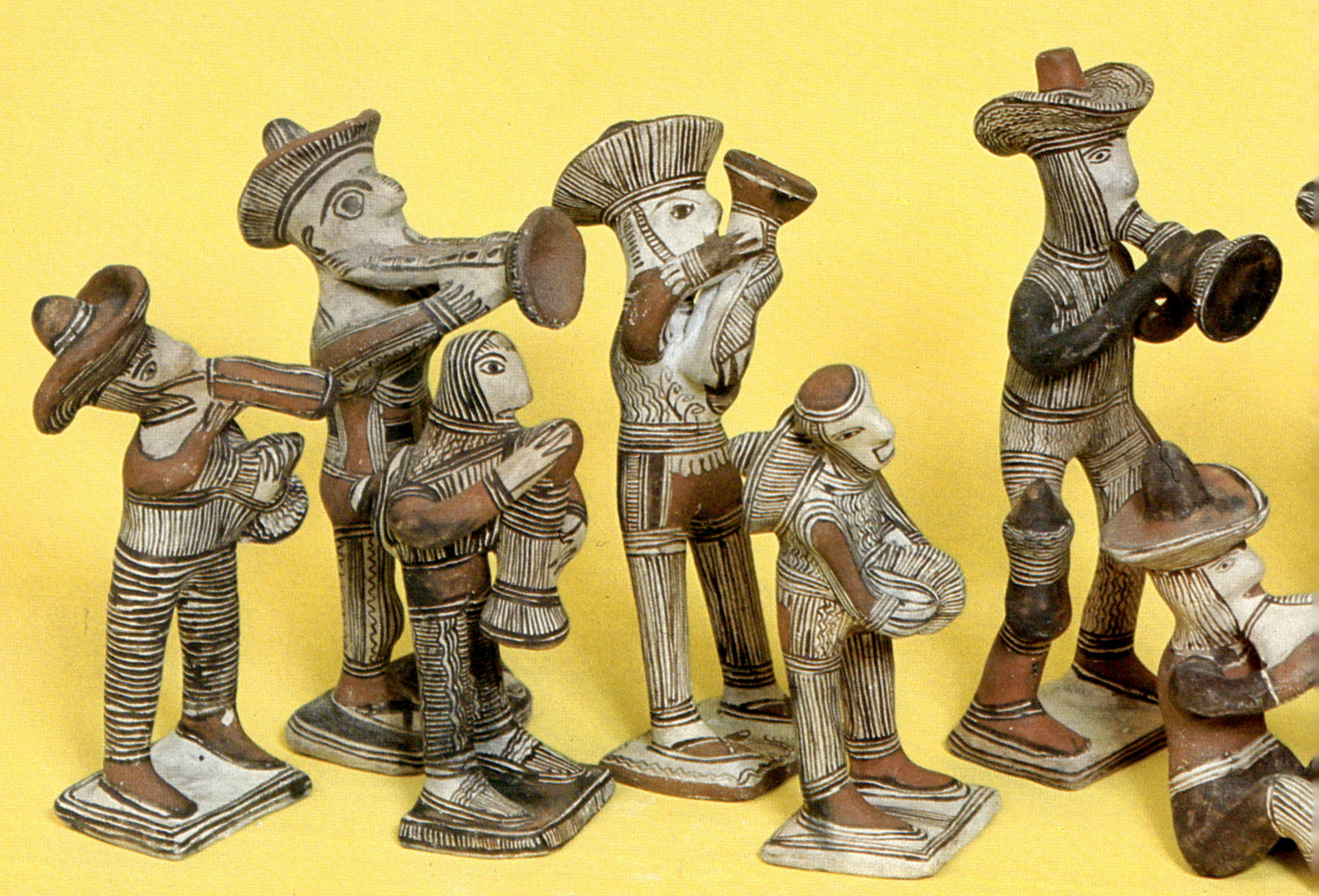

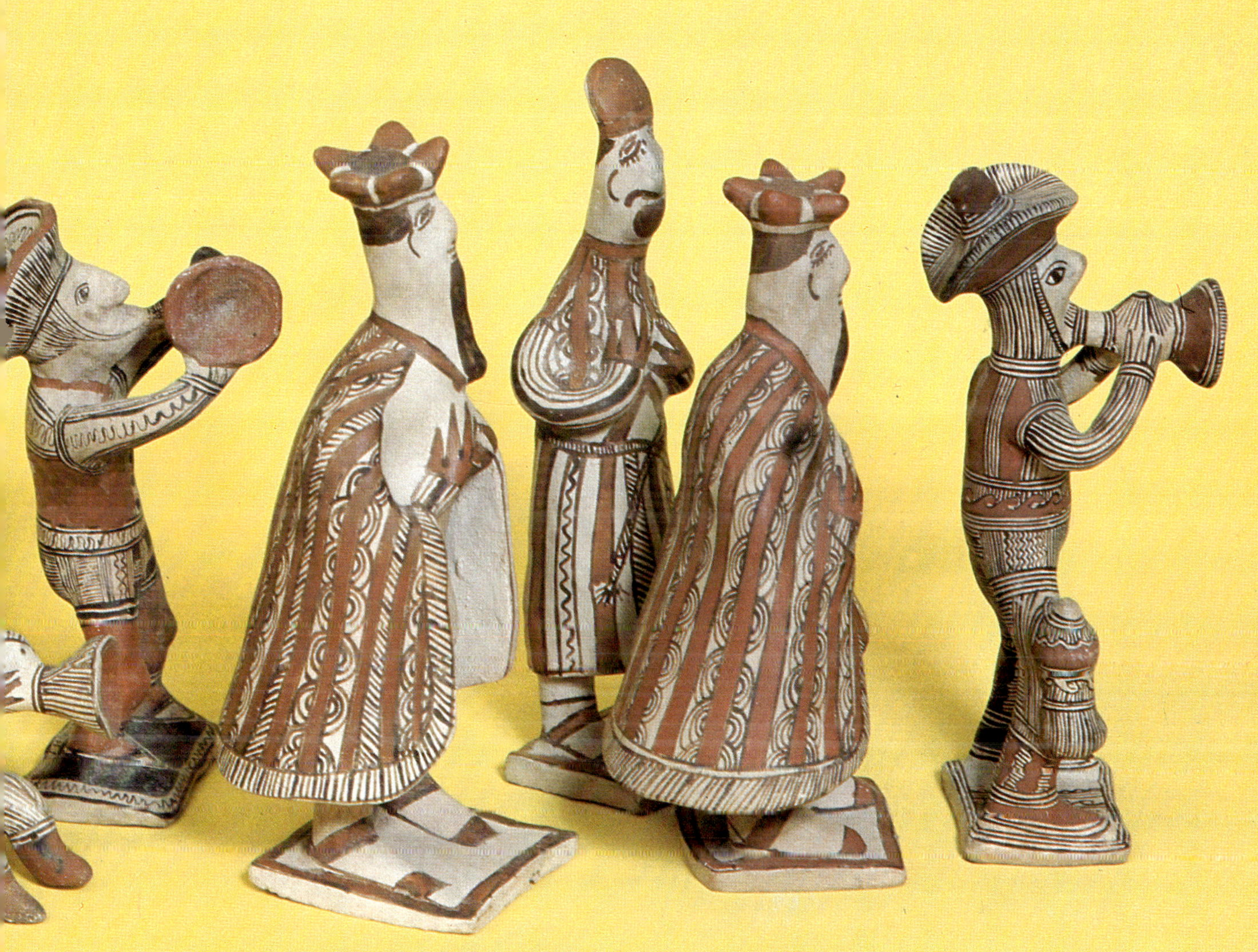

Preceding: *Three Kings with attendant musicians*, slip painted earthenware, San Agustín de las Flores, State of Guerrero, king 8″ high.

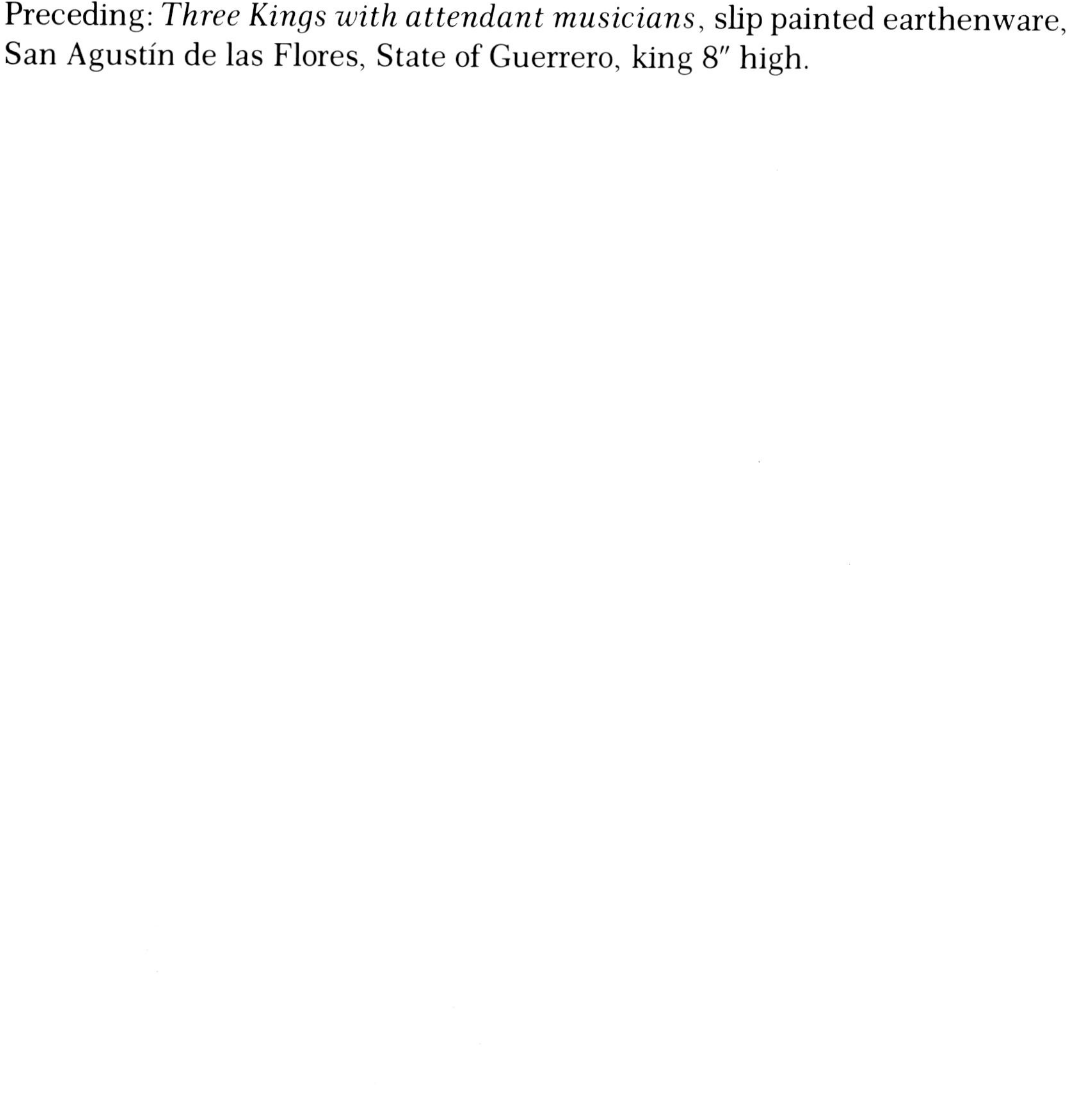

*Children's Toys*, clay, wood, hemp, tule and papier mache, various states of Mexico, ferris wheel 19-1/2″ high. The children of Mexico put their shoes out to be filled with toys and trinkets. They write letters to the kings rather than to Santa Claus.

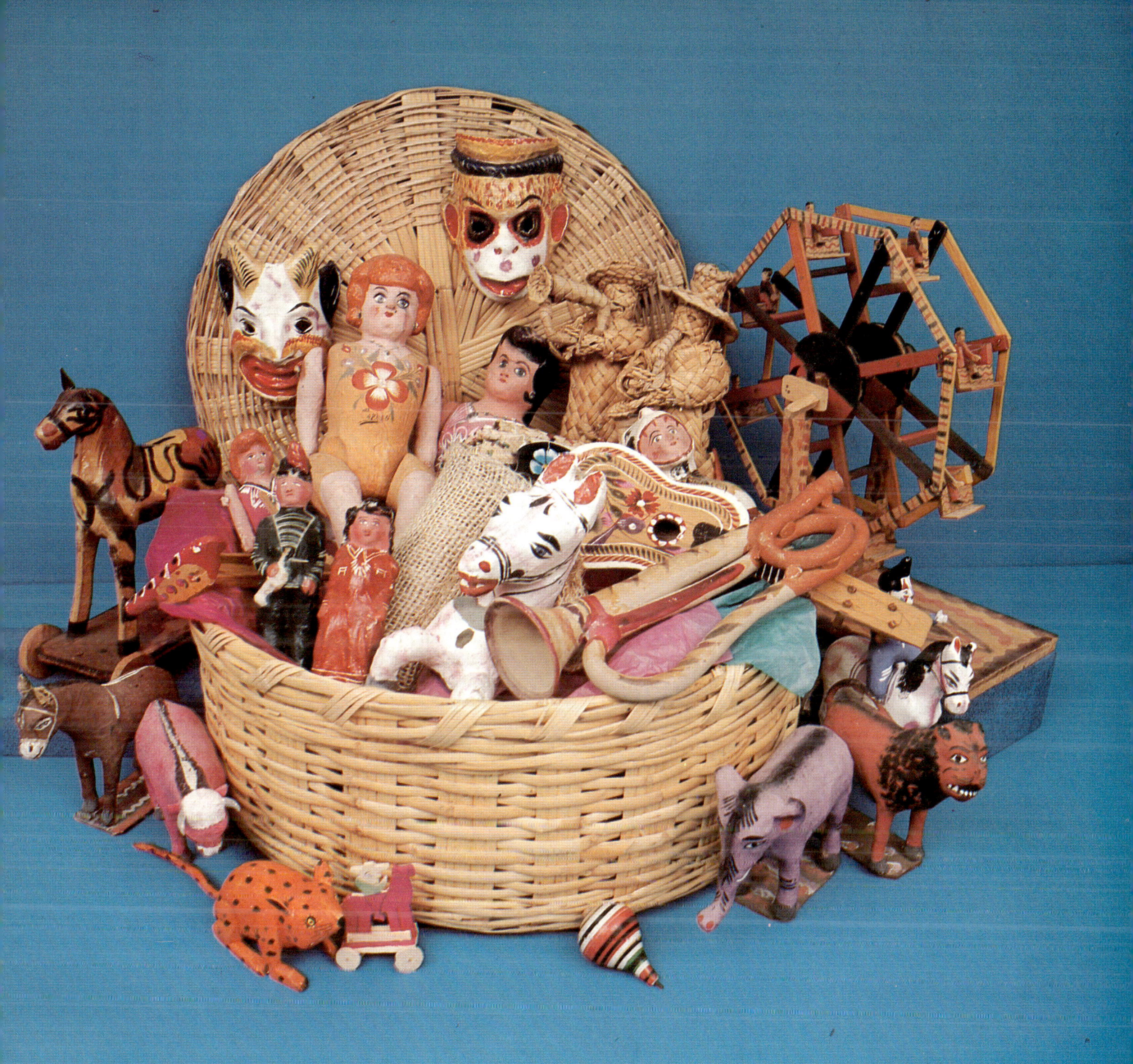

*Three Kings,* stained earthenware, Acatlán, State of Puebla, 14″ high. The representations of animals are often fantastic since models are not available.

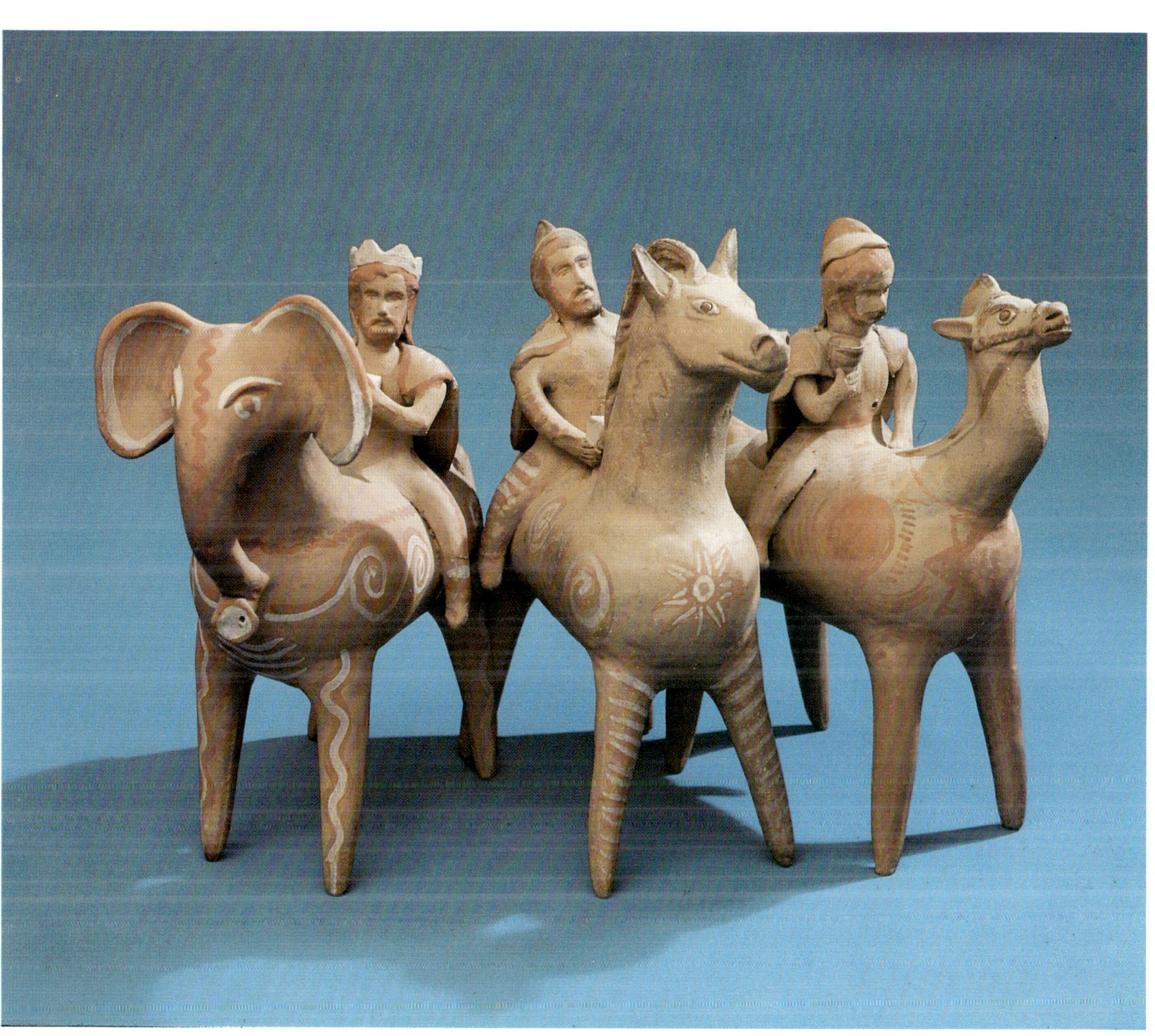

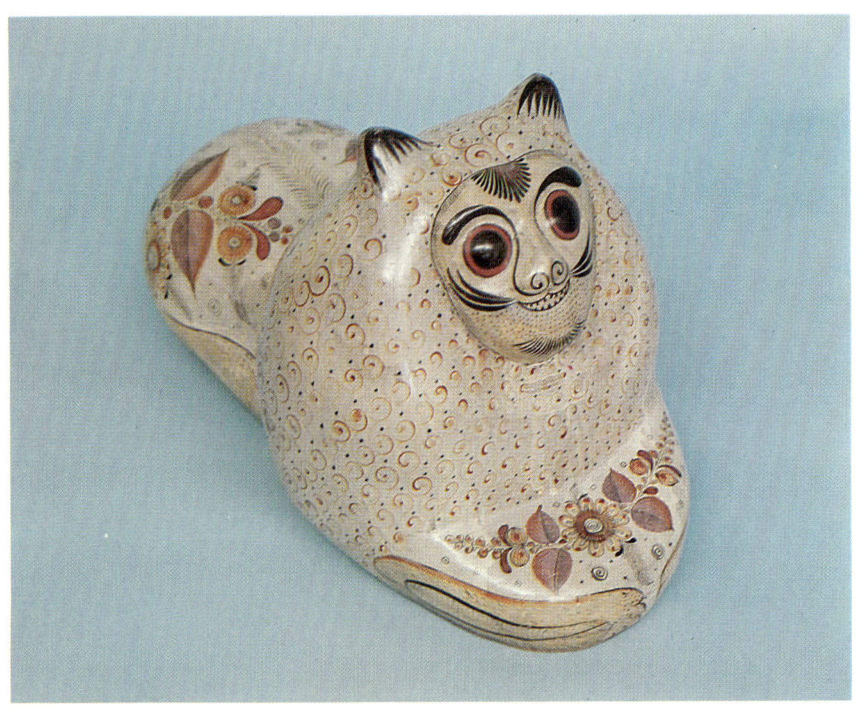

*Toy Lion*, slip painted and burnished terra cotta, Tonalá, State of Jalisco, 11″ high. The technique of making the pottery has remained the same since pre-conquest times.
*Toy Monkey*, earthenware, San Felipe, State of Guanajuato, 39″ high. Many of the toys of Mexico are made to be contemplated with joy but are not to be played with. This particular piece dates from the nineteenth century.

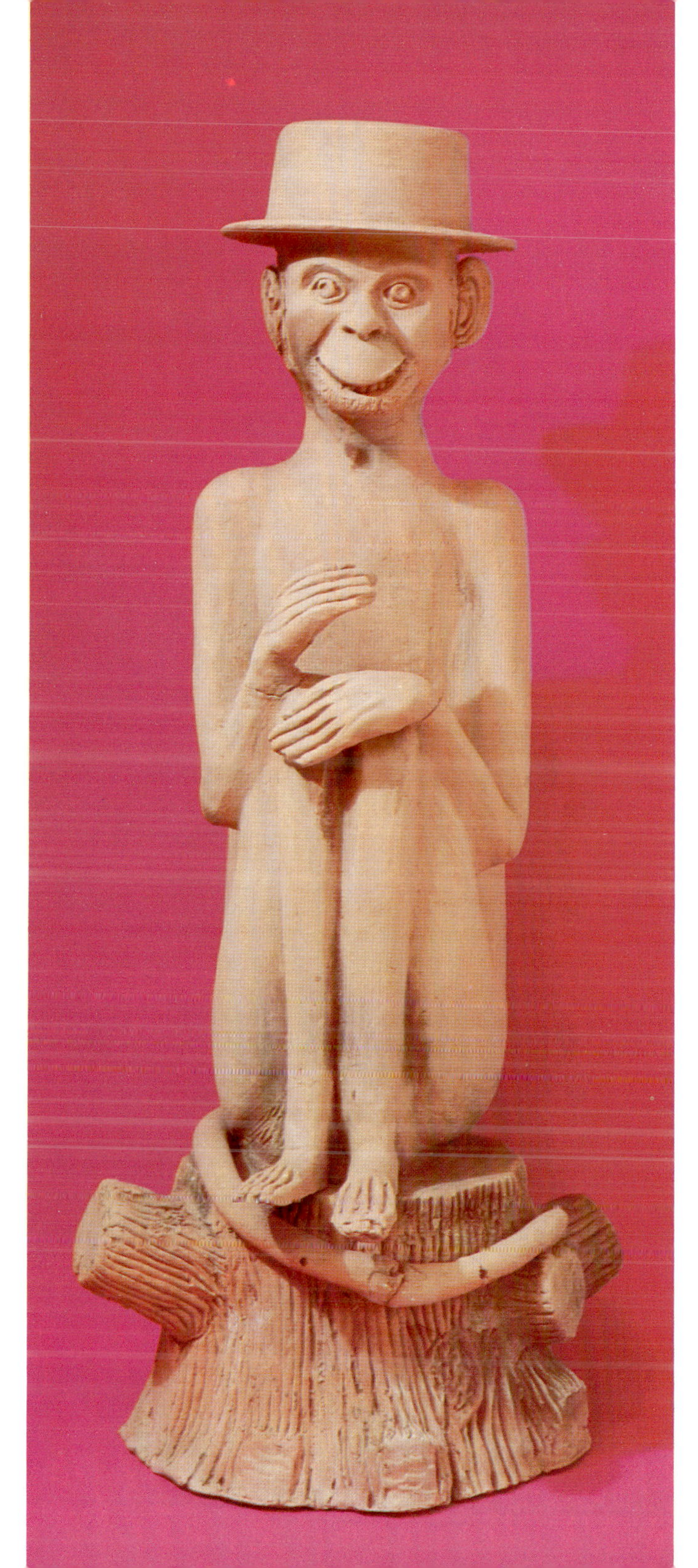

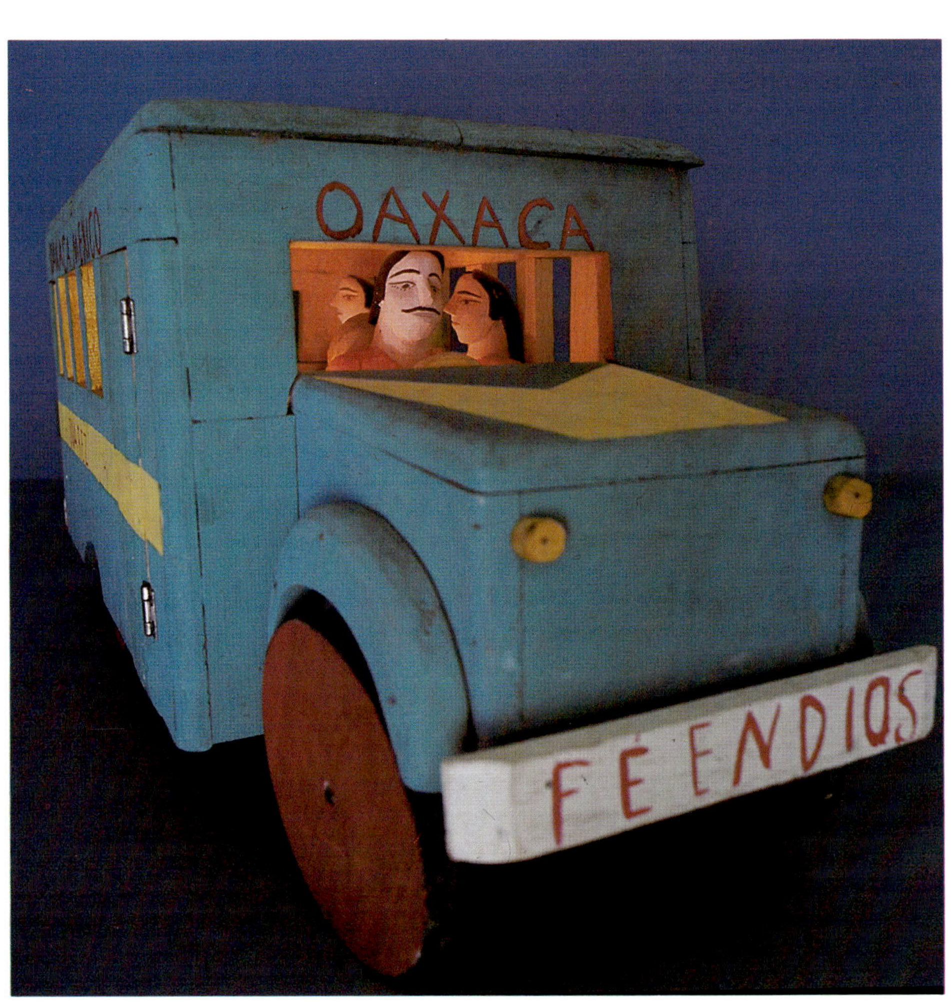
OAXACA
FÉ EN DIOS

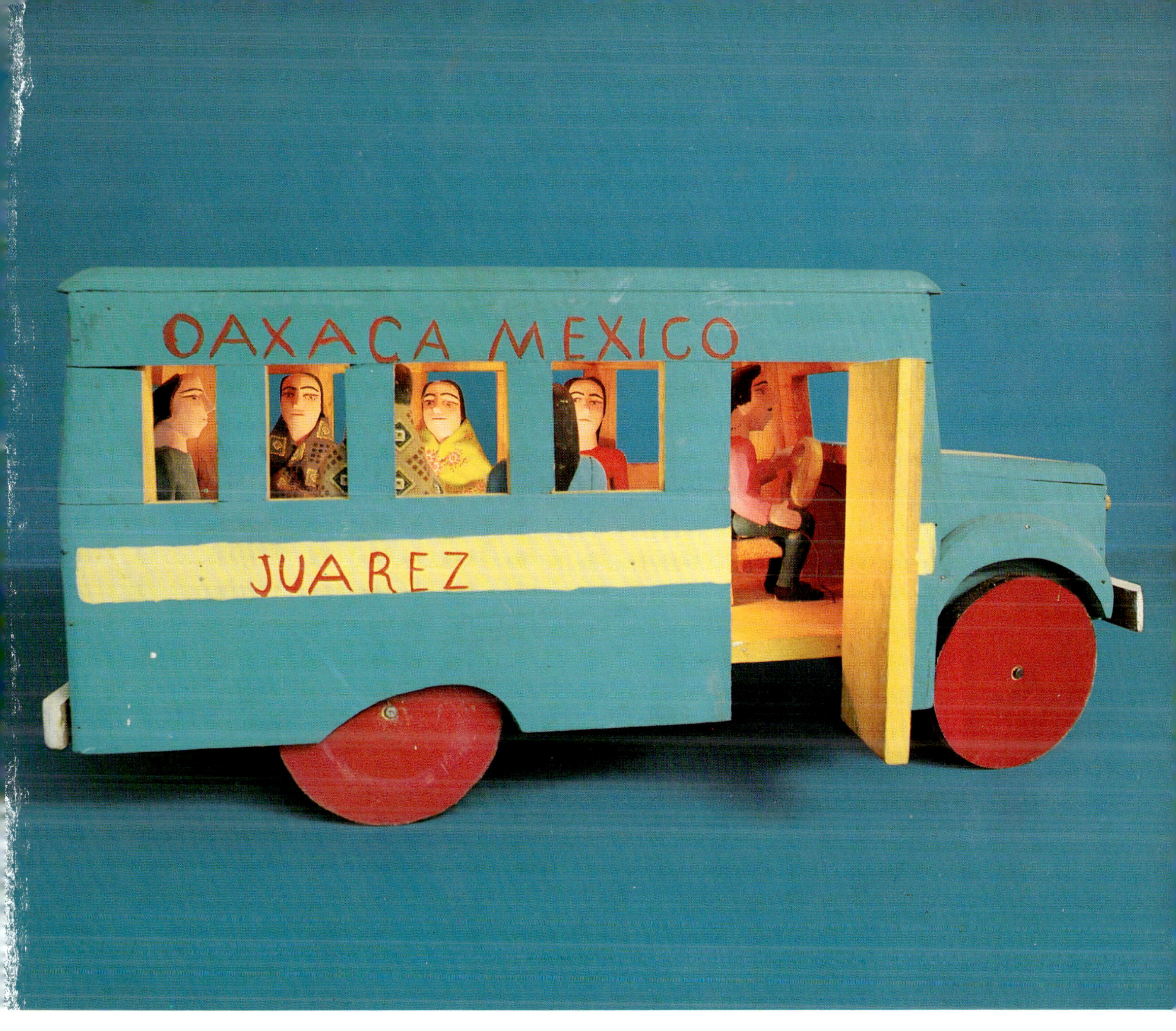


*Toy Bus*, painted and stained wood, Arrasola, State of Oaxaca, 15″ high.

# V. J. M. y J.

*February 2*

Candelmas and the Flight into Egypt. The end of the Christmas season.

*Flight into Egypt,* enameled terra cotta, Tlaquepaque, State of Jalisco, 12-1/2″ high. This piece is interesting in its advanced technique. Rather than being hand-painted, it shows the use of spray painting.

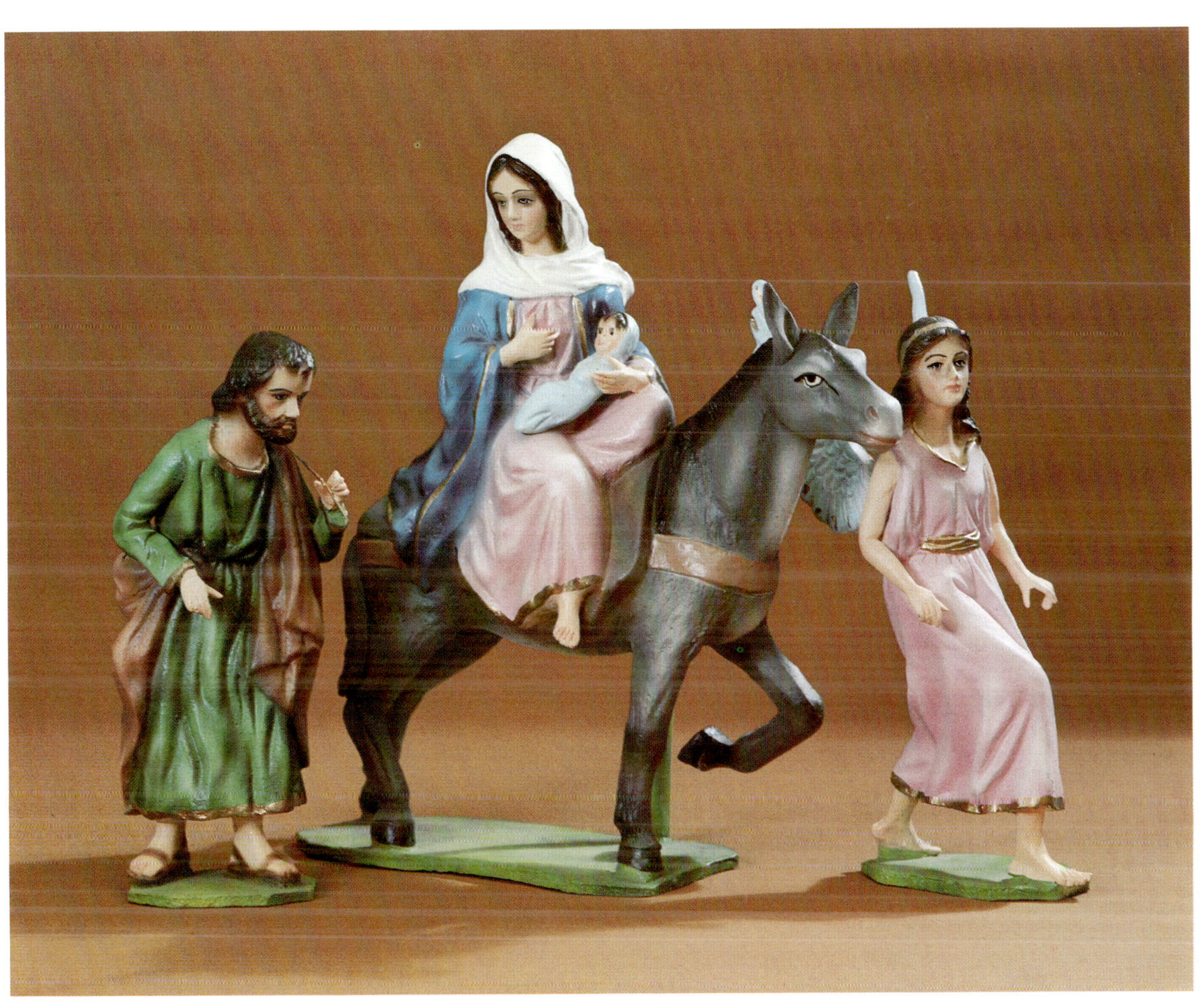

*Flight into Egypt,* painted earthenware, Acatlán, State of Puebla, 11″ high. The birds possibly represent the angels who protected the Holy Family on their journey.

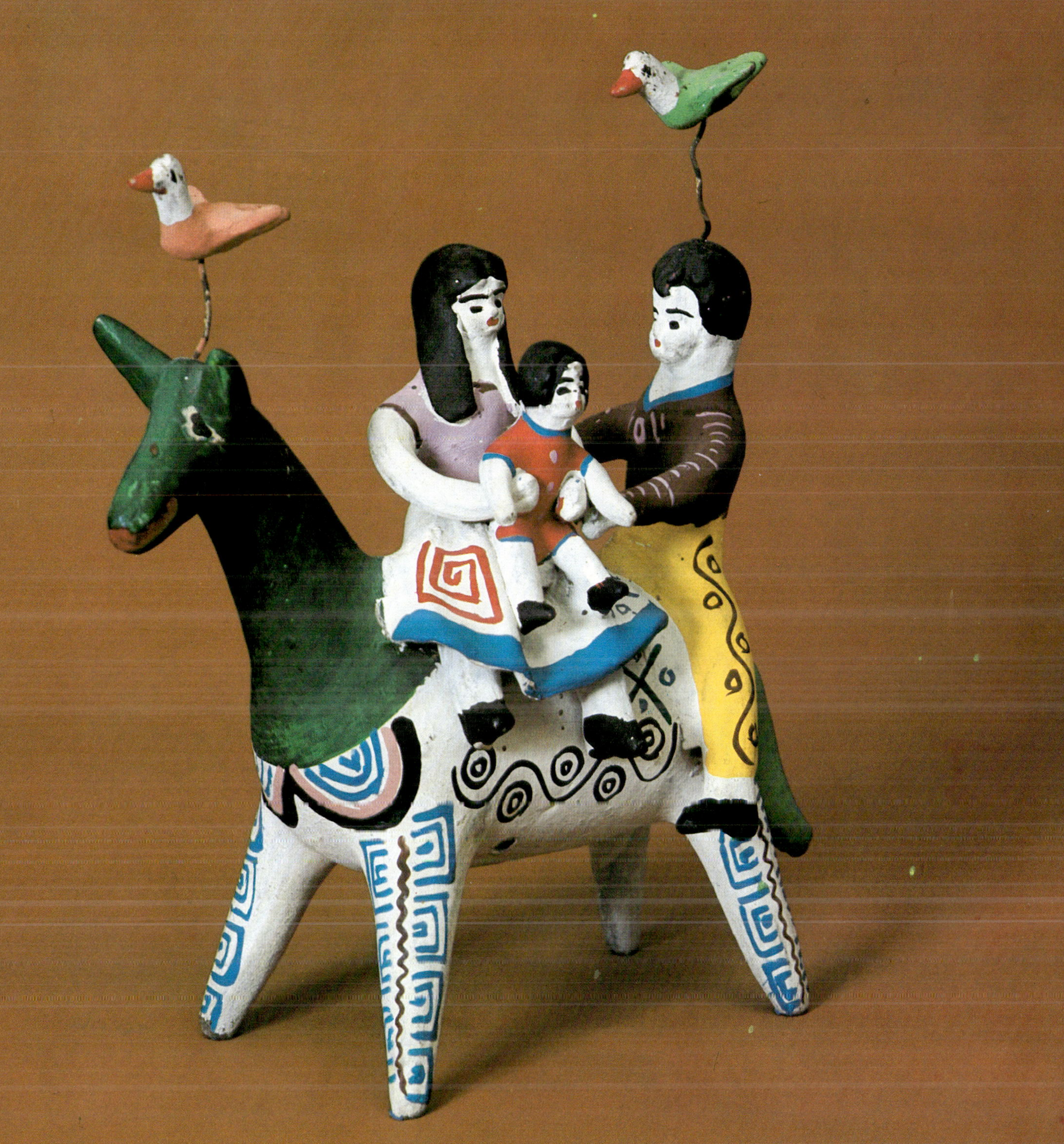

Map of Mexico showing villages and states mentioned in captions. The sun dial design is adapted from Tonalá pottery by Jorge Wilmot.

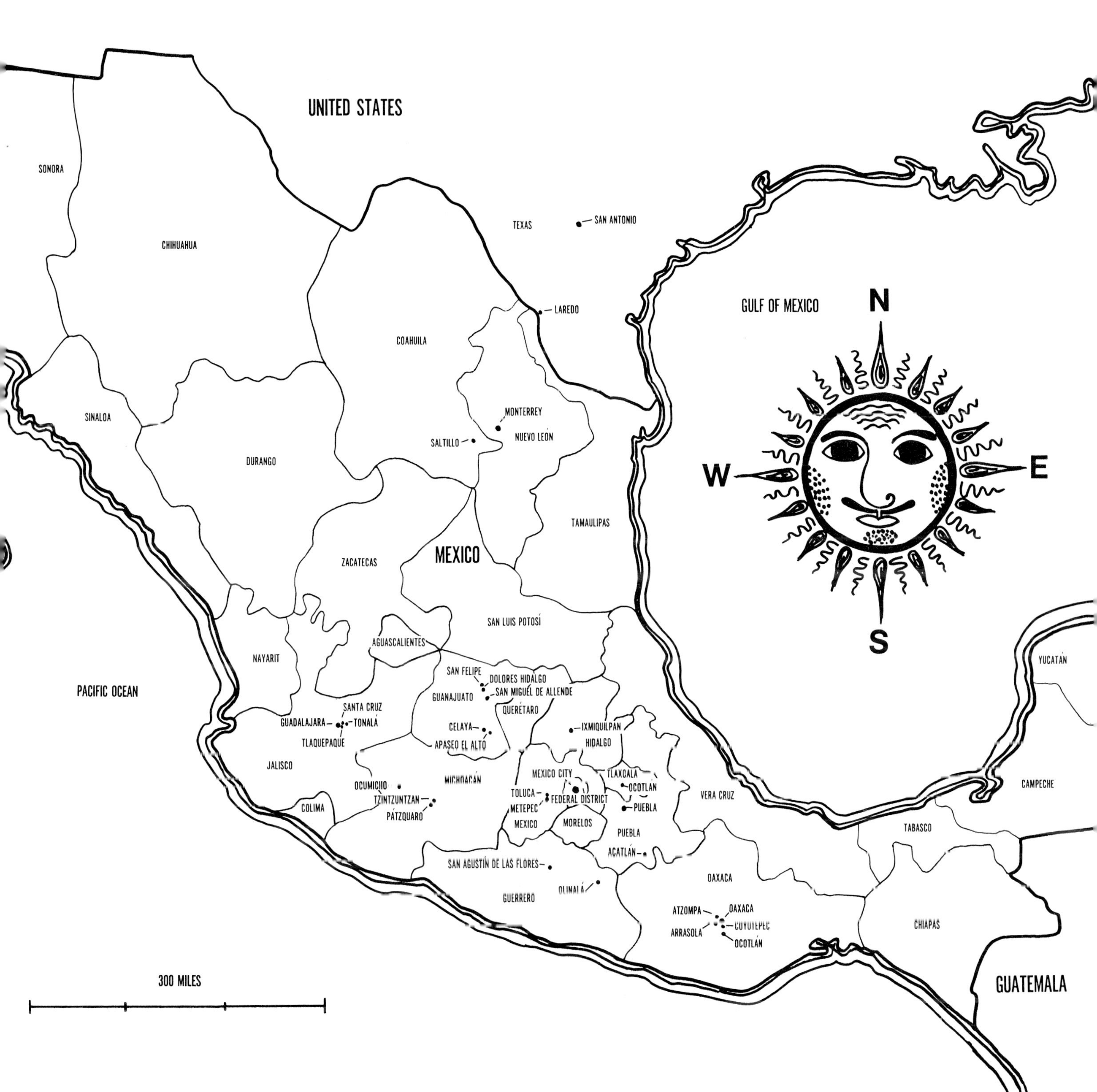

UNITED STATES
SONORA
CHIHUAHUA
TEXAS
SAN ANTONIO
LAREDO
COAHUILA
GULF OF MEXICO
N
W
E
S
SINALOA
MONTERREY
SALTILLO
NUEVO LEÓN
DURANGO
TAMAULIPAS
ZACATECAS
MEXICO
SAN LUIS POTOSÍ
AGUASCALIENTES
NAYARIT
YUCATÁN
PACIFIC OCEAN
SAN FELIPE
DOLORES HIDALGO
GUANAJUATO
SAN MIGUEL DE ALLENDE
QUERÉTARO
SANTA CRUZ
GUADALAJARA
TONALÁ
TLAQUEPAQUE
CELAYA
APASEO EL ALTO
IXMIQUILPAN
HIDALGO
JALISCO
OCUMICHO
MICHOACÁN
MEXICO CITY
TLAXCALA
OCOTLÁN
TOLUCA
FEDERAL DISTRICT
PUEBLA
TZINTZUNTZAN
PÁTZQUARO
METEPEC
MEXICO
MORELOS
VERA CRUZ
CAMPECHE
COLIMA
TABASCO
PUEBLA
ACATLÁN
SAN AGUSTÍN DE LAS FLORES
OAXACA
OLINALÁ
GUERRERO
ATZOMPA
OAXACA
COYOTEPEC
ARRASOLA
OCOTLÁN
CHIAPAS
300 MILES
GUATEMALA

# Glossary

*appliqued design.* Laid on pellets and "snakes" of clay attached with pressure and slip.

*black clay.* From Oaxaca. Cow dung is used in firing, creating heavy smoke. The black pottery from Acatlán, Puebla, is treated with graphite.

*burnished.* An unfired leather-hard ceramic is polished with a smooth stone, closing the pores of the clay and creating a shiny surface.

*"Coke" bottle glass.* The glass of the "Coke" bottle of Mexico was a soft fire glass and could be recycled into new pieces.

*Colonial.* Indicating that an object was made in the nineteenth century or earlier.

*earthenware.* Beige (tan) colored clay.

*enameled.* Painted with household oil paint.

*gilded.* Gold leaf applied on gesso (a mixture of plaster and glue).

*glazed.* Pottery overlaid with a thin surface consisting of glass.

*hemp.* Dried fibers of the maguey (century plant).

*painted.* A water-based paint, occasionally varnished.

*papier mache.* Paper mixed or coated with paste.

*polychromed.* Multicolor painting on gesso.

*slip.* Clay in liquid state applied with brush or by dipping.

*stained.* A very thin color applied to bamboo, palm, wood, and clay.

*terra cotta.* Red-brown colored clay.

*tule.* Cattail reed found in the lake areas.

# *Bibliography*


Arellano Garza, Humberto. "Arts and Crafts in Mexico." *Texas Quarterly* 2 (Spring 1959): 156–167.

"Arte Popular y Artesanias de Mexico." *Artes de Mexico* Números 43/44 (1962).

Caso, Alfonso. "El Arte Popular Mexicano." *Mexico in el Arte* Número 12 (Nov. 1952): 87–100.

Crawford, William, Jr. *Time is a Holiday*. New York: Oxford University Press, 1951.

"El Arte Popular de Mexico." Artes de Mexico Número Extraordinario (1970–1971).

Niggli, Josefina. *A Miracle for Mexico*. Greenwich, Conn: New York Graphic Society Publishers, Ltd., 1964.

Norman, James, and Margaret Fox Schmidt. *A Shopper's Guide to Mexico: Where, What and How to Buy*. Garden City, N.Y.: Doubleday and Company, Inc., 1973.

Norman, James. *Terry's Guide to Mexico*. Garden City, N.Y.: Doubleday and Company, Inc., 1962.

Ross, Patricia Fent. *Made in Mexico*. New York: Alfred A. Knopf, 1960.

Villegas, Victor Manuel. *Arte Popular de Guanajuato*. Published by Banco National de Fomento Cooperativo, Sociedad Anónima, de C, V, Mexico, 1964.

"Virgenes de Mexico." *Artes de Mexico* Número 113 (1968).

Waugh, Julia Nott. *The Silver Cradle*. Austin: University of Texas Press, 1955.

Robert K. Winn is an artist craftsman, collector and student of Mexican regional dress and folk art, author, lecturer, consultant, and designer. Since the 1940's, Mr. Winn has been collecting Mexican folk art, particularly relating to Christmas, and in 1972 designed and executed the Mexican Christmas Exhibit for the Art Museum of South Texas, Corpus Christi, displaying his own collection. Fifty thousand visitors attended this exhibit in one month. The same exhibit was at the McNay Museum, San Antonio, in 1975, and will be at the Lyndon Baines Johnson Library, Austin, in 1977.

Because of his outstanding achievements in the community, a Testimonial Fiesta in his honor was held in San Antonio in 1973, at which time he received a citation for special service to the City by the San Antonio City Council, was made Ambassador-at-Large, San Antonio Chamber of Commerce and Almirante by the Paseo del Rio Association, received a Distinguished Achievement Award from the San Antonio Museum Association, and many other similar honors.

Mr. Winn received his M.A. degree in Fine and Industrial Arts from Columbia University in New York. As an artist-craftsman, he works in mosaic, enameling, sculpture, and jewelry. He has executed commissions in enamel on copper for churches in Midland, San Angelo, and San Antonio, and a major work in sculpture in Bandera for the architect, the late Henry Steinbomer. He is represented in the Liturgical Art Collection of the Episcopal Diocese in San Antonio with a stone figure of St. Francis. Mr. Winn is presently Exhibit Consultant for United Services Automobile Association and curator of the City Water Board Water Museum.

Mr. Winn was one of the contributors to the book, *San Antonio in the Eighteenth Century,* published in 1976 by the Bicentennial Historical Committee.

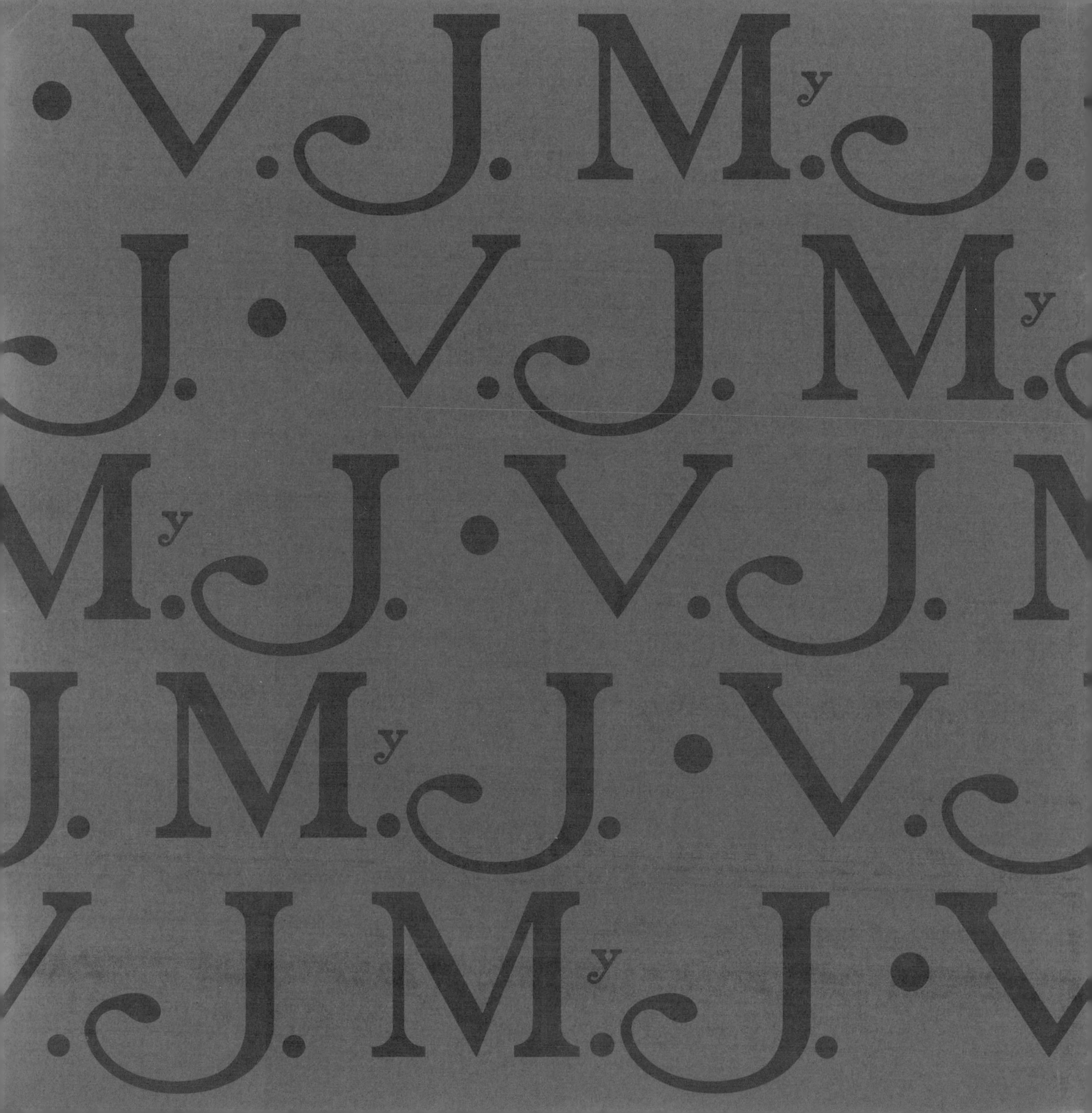